DUKE IT OUT

DUKE IT OUT

Exploring Three Principles of a Successful Life

By Roy Duke Nyberg

Copyright © 2010
Rodora Nyberg

ALL RIGHTS RESERVED
This work may not be used in any form,
or reproduced by any means,
in whole or in part,
without written permission
from the publisher.

ISBN: 978-1-57579-432-7

Library of Congress Control Number: 2010935736

Printed in the United States of America

PINE HILL PRESS
4000 West 57th Street
Sioux Falls, SD 57106

To my family for their love and support

To my relatives and friends who contributed
information and pictures

TABLE OF CONTENTS

Introduction

1. The Melding of Two Cultures 1
2. Exploring the Neighborhood and Peddling Papers 9
3. Scouting, Ace and Women 17
4. School Days and Teen Activities 25
5. World Events Change My Life 31
6. Army Life Begins 33
7. Two-and-a-Half Cents an Hour, 24-7 41
8. My First and True love 49
9. From a Honeymoon to Hibbing 57
10. Firearms and a Detour 61
11. Fourteen Years from Dream to Reality 67
12. That's the Way We Planned It 73
13. Triumph and Tragedy, 1969-1972 81
14. Changing with the Times 89
15. State and National Involvement 95
16. A Family of Six 103
17. Friends and Neighbors 115
18. Politics and Other Activities 121
19. The Big Sioux River 127
20. Retirement and Travel 135
21. The Kids Take a Turn 141

Final Thoughts
Epilogue
Photo Gallery

INTRODUCTION

One day my son, Kevin, said to me, "Dad, you have to write about the things you have experienced in your life and your success in business."

I knew what he meant. I began my working life as a six-year-old boy, selling the Sunday newspaper from door to door. When I retired at age 62 it was as the owner of an Ace Hardware store in Sioux Falls that had expanded from 4,000 square feet to a new location with 26,000 square feet in less than 20 years. Along the way, I have led professional organizations, taken part in community activities, and assisted many young people to get their start in business. In my private life I enjoyed a happy marriage with my wife, Rodora, and we raised four children.

Would people be interested in that? It's not easy, you know, to automatically assume people want to hear what you have to say. But as I thought about it and began to jog my memory for stories that might interest others, I kept coming back to a plain, plastic, wood-grain sign that I had in my office for many years. It now hangs on a wall in my home.

It lists the three principles that I think can make your life successful, particularly if you start following them in your earliest years. They are the guiding forces behind how my parents raised me, consciously or not, and how Rodora and I raised our children and now serve as models for our nine grandchildren to follow, again consciously or not.

The three principles are *environment*, *exposure* and *involvement*.

The first, *environment*, may seem like something we cannot control. For instance, I am the son of an immigrant father and a Tennessee-born mother and was raised in one of Minnesota's northernmost counties. It was an area that still had no roads a mere decade before I was born. My birth came just prior to the start of the Depression. The values instilled in me during a time of financial devastation were survival, conservation and conservatism. I was in my early teens when World War II began, and the possibility that I might find myself in battle was one that haunted me through high school.

But *environment* also means the role models who surround you, such as your playmates, your teachers, and other adults who take an interest in molding young minds. Because many men went off to fight in the war, my early business models were the five women who ran the hardware store in International Falls. I was surrounded by and trained by women. I was fortunate to grow up in an *environment* where god-fearing adults helped shape my character.

Exposure comes from a willingness to try different things. For me, Boy Scouts provided an *exposure* to many different activities and interests. Helping support my family through the pennies I earned from that early paper route showed me how important it was that I looked beyond my own wants and needs. In Miss Agnes Pirkl's "commercial" classes at Falls High School, I looked beyond the temporary embarrassment of being the only boy learning bookkeeping to prepare myself for a future in business.

Involvement goes beyond one's professional life. My years as a Boy Scout established a determination and confidence that allowed me to undertake any reasonable or practical dream or venture. As I grew older, I plunged into a variety of clubs and organizations, many of which had the goal of improving others' lives.

As you read this book, I hope you see how *environment, exposure* and *involvement* have played a role in my life and will use these examples when looking at your own life.

You also will see how influential an organization such as Scouting can be on a young person's life. As I look back on it, I understand that the virtues I learned as a young Boy Scout growing up in International Falls shaped my life. Trustworthiness, loyalty, helpfulness, friendliness, courtesy, kindness, obedience, cheerfulness, thriftiness, bravery, cleanliness and reverence: Is there a better pattern for living one's life?

As a boy, I never realized the impact that those people around me, the decisions I made, and the activities I chose to participate in would have in the years to come. With this book, I hope to inspire others to realize how *environment*, *exposure* and *involvement* have shaped them in the past and will shape them in the future.

Roy Duke Nyberg

Chapter 1
THE MELDING OF TWO CULTURES

My parents moved to the town that was to be their home for decades when they were both young.

My father was 19 on November 11, 1916, the day he landed at Ellis Island, New York, having left his home in Hammer, Torsaker, Sweden, less than two weeks earlier, then boarding the S.S. Kristianiafjord in Bergen, Norway. I often have wondered what it must have been like for my father to say goodbye to his parents, knowing it was highly likely he never would see them again. That's what happened. Dad returned to his boyhood home in the 1960s, but his parents had died by then.

In 1913, my mother was only nine years old when she left her birthplace of Cookeville, Tennessee, with her mother and her siblings to join her father for a new life in northern Minnesota. It was a stressful time, and Mother told my younger brother that her mother told her children if they cried during the move, "she would give us a licking."

Nils Otto Nyberg and Helen Ruth Wirt settled separately in International Falls, the county seat of Koochiching County, Minnesota. They met when Mother was a junior in high school and Dad, eight years older, already was hard at work in the mills.

The part of Minnesota they moved to, right across the border from Canada, was a good place for young people in the early 20th century. It too was young since Koochiching County itself wasn't settled until the 1880s and didn't become a separate government unit until 1906.

The first rail lines to International Falls weren't built until that year. Even 15 years before I was born the roads in the county were few and difficult to traverse. A 1912 Koochiching County map describes 80 percent of the land as swamp, and only 108 miles of roads existed. Putting any kind of surface on the roads – even just gravel – didn't begin until 1917. It was in 1926, the year that I was born, that a Minnesota highway commissioner vowed that state roads would be kept open all winter – the first time that ever had been attempted.

Residents had voted to split off from Itasca County partly because of the difficulties in having its county seat, Grand Rapids, "only" 130 miles away as the crow flies with no passable roads and a staggering 400 miles away by railway. But they also showed an independence and a pioneer spirit, one fostered by an *environment* that discouraged farming and soon showed that the large stands of pine and other trees such as spruce, balsam and cedar largely would provide the residents' livelihood through logging, sawmills, planing mills and the production of paper.

The climate also shaped the early residents who proved hardy enough to withstand lows of -50° with summer temperatures that would climb to the upper 90s (although the 100° mark never has been reached).

My father, who was known to family and friends as Otto, had left Sweden to join other family members, including a brother in International Falls. My mother, Helen, also had extended family in the area when she moved there.

The weather adjustment must have been greater for my mother than my father, who came from a more similar climate in Sweden. My mother's family had lived for generations in eastern Tennessee. She told me several times that it was customary for the children in her family to be nursed by the "colored" servants that the Duke family employed.

Her mother, Jessie Lou Duke, had married Walter Wirt, and they became the parents of eight children. Mother's younger sister, Mabel, died when Mom still was living at home, a loss she spoke of frequently; her older brother, Duke, died when she was pregnant with me. My middle name, Duke, was a tribute to that side of the family. Early in life I discouraged "Duke" from being used as my nickname, however, since when I was a boy many neighborhood dogs bore that name.

My father was born on New Year's Day in 1897. Family names on his side are Wikner and Eskilsson; my grandfather kept the name Nyberg, which means "new mountain" in Swedish, when others in his family changed names.

The first of my father's brothers to leave Sweden did so in 1902. My family history was shaped by the fact that Norway earned its independence from Sweden in 1905. In my family, at least, young men who didn't want to be part of an involuntary conscription and worried that the tension between the two countries could lead to war and left to establish a home elsewhere. There were other reasons, too. Dad once told my brother, Bob, that he left Sweden to keep from starving to death. Seven of my dad's eight brothers lived to adulthood; five came to the United States, with four settling in Minnesota and one in Wisconsin.

My father actually left Sweden illegally to come to the United States. The village pastor had to give permission before someone could leave for America, and he did that for one of Dad's older brothers. That brother tucked those papers in a suit pocket and sent it back home. Then a second brother came over; in turn, he sent the papers back to the third brother. My brother, Bob, says Dad was the fourth brother to use those papers to leave Sweden, and one brother came over after him. My father emigrated with his younger sister, Esther, and a male cousin. None of them could speak a word of English. But once Dad learned English, he never spoke Swedish again. Some of my Nyberg cousins couldn't speak English when we went to school, but Dad would have none of that.

What little I know about what my father's life must have been like in Sweden comes from a first cousin, Evert Ekbergh, who also emigrated to the United States as a young man. He grew up on my grandparents' home place. Dad attended school in Sweden only through the eighth grade; after that he began working in a sawmill. Life with 13 children on a farm in south-central Sweden was hard.

He began learning English in Hayward, Wisconsin, where he first settled. Dad next moved to Minneapolis, then left for Seattle. The United States had entered World War I, and while Dad couldn't speak English well enough to enter the service, he did his part and worked in the shipyards. After that, he moved to International Falls.

How my parents met I am not sure, but I think it's likely that it was at a dance. My father loved to dance, as do I, and it was one of the most popular activities then among young people. He was a member of the Odd Fellows, the Moose and the Elks lodges, and all three held frequent dances and card parties. My mother told my brother, Bob, that no one thought it was unusual that a girl only a junior in high school would date a man eight years her senior.

My mother was 19 when she finished her schooling on June 4, 1924, part of the first class to graduate from the new high school building in International Falls, and 20 at the time of her marriage on June 23, 1925. My father was 28. They were married on Mother's Grandma Catherine Wirt's 85th birthday.

Almost ten months later, on April 17, 1926, I was born at Craig Hospital in International Falls. My first name was chosen, my mother said, just because they liked it. My brother, Robert, who always was known as Bob, completed the family exactly 4½ years later, on October 17, 1930. In between us boys, Mother had a miscarriage. Had the baby lived, I would have had a sister.

My father spent his working life in the mills, the sawmill first, then the planing mill until it closed shortly before World War II began. He also worked in the paper mill. Even during the Depression, he worked long days, six days a week, but the pay wasn't much for a family of four. I only saw him cry twice in my life. Once was when he realized that a $10 bill had fallen out unnoticed when he pulled his hands from his pocket. That was a financial blow.

Dad was an amazingly talented millwright, a craftsman who specialized in building and maintaining equipment. He could splice rope so expertly that you couldn't see where two ropes had become one. I still have boxes of his tools, some of which he made himself. I think Bob inherited Dad's ability to work with his hands, or maybe it was because family finances weren't as bleak when Bob was in his teens and Dad had more time to spend with him. Whether because of hereditary or *exposure*, I don't have the same gift.

But Dad also was creative, a quite imaginative man. I do think I got that from him, as have some of my children.

In addition to his skill as a millwright, Dad had an entrepreneurial spirit and always looked for other ways to make his fortune. One of those enterprises led to operating a resort on Lake Kabetogama known as Gappes Landing. The resort included garages where people from the Twin Cities could leave their cars in storage while they vacationed and a combination cafe/bar.

It was strictly a summertime proposition, but since my father continued to work at the mill in International Falls, the task of running it fell to Mother. She became chief cook and bottle-washer for the dinette. It was a hard life for her. I remember once the gas stove blew up, the force crashing her against a wall. Fortunately, she was not badly injured.

The resort also provided employment for me as I become *involved* in the family enterprises. I learned how to filet the fish vacationers caught. I hand-pumped gasoline into an old-fashioned vertical pump with a globe on top; from that pump the gas was dispensed into cars and containers. Because of the bar, I also had my first taste of Miller Genuine Draft Beer when I was 14 years old!

Mother showed little enthusiasm for many of Dad's schemes and projects. She was raised by a woman who was very much a Southern belle. Her mother – we kids called her Granny – was only one generation removed from the Civil War. Granny expected her children to wait on her. She was unhappy with the move to International Falls and regretted it the rest of her life. My mother had wanted to be a nurse, but Granny wouldn't allow it, saying it was a disgusting profession for a woman. Again, nurses didn't gain respectability until the Civil War and for some people it took even longer to forget the stereotypes.

I don't think marriage to an immigrant with limited education and multiple schemes to make money was the life Granny had envisioned for her daughter or that Mother had envisioned for herself. Mother and Dad came from drastically different backgrounds: Dad a Swedish immigrant, Mother from a family that can trace its roots in this country back to 1640. That's 20 years after the landing of the Pilgrims at Plymouth Rock! And there is a picture of a Wirt, her father's family, hanging on a wall at Independence Hall in Philadelphia.

My father was a practical joker, light-hearted and fun-loving. For years he carried a cigarette lighter that said, "Once a knight, always a knight … but once a night's enough." Although he had a good sense of humor, when he fixed his penetrating eyes on you, whatever prank you were up to came to an abrupt end.

He loved to garden, although his main crop was raspberries from bushes he planted in the backyard. In 1936, when I was a boy, he purchased land on Rainy Lake, seven miles from town, where he built a cabin. In Sweden, it was customary to have a summer house in the country, and Dad followed that tradition, despite the fact it was the Depression. He wasn't working even 40 hours a week at the mill when times became tough, and my brother had to wear my hand-me-down clothing. Dad only paid $50 for all the wood necessary to build the cabin. He used leftover rough-cut wood from the sawmill and planed and finished the wood himself.

The first road in the area wasn't built until 1935, and our property was half a mile from that. Dad and I cut the road to our driveway. Because Dad began building before there were any roads, he floated the housing materials on a flat-bottomed boat, loading it so heavily that it was only inches above the lake water. I was with him, and I remember it clearly because riding in a boat so low in the water scared me. We would fish from that boat, and we also fished from Finlanders Point, casting our lines into the waters of Rainy Lake.

One time, my father was going fishing with my Uncle Jim, who was married to one of Mother's sisters. Uncle Jim brought up a brand-new fishing rod that had cost $25. Dad was fishing with a yellow chalk line tied to the boat's gunnel, just simple equipment. But he caught one fish after another, while Uncle Jim didn't even get a bite. My uncle became so frustrated, he literally tossed the whole rod and reel into the lake. Uncle Jim, by the way, had a famous niece: the late evangelist and television personality Tammy Faye Bakker Messner, who was born in International Falls in 1942.

Dad spent hours clearing boulders from the beach. He would use a five-foot metal bar to pry up a boulder, then stick logs under it to keep it from sinking back down. That is when my brother, Bob, learned a lesson from Dad that has stuck with him: Don't work harder, work smarter.

The boulder and other rocks would be used to protect the shoreline so waves wouldn't erode it. Dad also used logs that had broken away from the tugboats towing them down to the mill. The waves then pushed the logs to shore.

Mother viewed the cabin as an escape from everyday life, Bob says. She enjoyed having relatives and friends come visit. She entertained frequently in town, but guests coming to Rainy Lake was even better.

In later years, Dad taught my four children how to pick wild blueberries from low-lying bushes behind the cabin. That is one of their most vivid memories of my father, who died in 1969 when he was 72 years old. The lot today is owned by Bob, who has replaced one of the two original cabins with a larger home. And he says the blueberry bushes are mostly gone.

My mother's side of the family valued education. Grandfather Wirt had worked in a printing shop, then ran a coal and feed business. He no longer had that business when his brother, my great-uncle Charlie, asked him to move to International Falls to help operate a grocery and dry goods store he planned to build. Uncle Charlie also owned a confectionery.

I am closer to my father's relatives in Sweden than I am to my mother's family. I remember going to Tennessee in 1942, and a distant cousin wanted to re-fight the Civil War. Literally! They also called me, more than once, a "damn Yankee." That experience was so unpleasant it soured me on that side of the family. During that visit I met my great-grandmother who was in her late 90s. She had been a young women during the Civil War and had relatives who fought for the South.

Mother was a great woman. She always dressed neatly and kept a spotless house. My daughter Nancy calls my mother "a classy lady." She helped supplement the family finances during the Depression by going door to door with me selling Christmas cards, earning forty cents for every dollar's worth of cards we sold. Later on, she was employed with the local J.C. Penney department store and showed a knack for that, becoming a top saleswoman.

But in her 40s, Mother developed a depression that eventually required shock treatments, the favored procedure of the time. She would travel to Duluth for the procedures. Dad and his entrepreneurial efforts that never made the fortune he envisioned had put a lot of stress on Mother, as did the moving we did in my teen years from one house to another. We lived in three locations during my high school years. Mother couldn't have her nice things with her. Dad once built a lean-to at the lake home to store her furniture. The rain came through the roof and ruined everything.

At one point they lived in tourist cabins. I was embarrassed when I brought Rodora to International Falls to meet my folks, and she had to see where they lived.

When she was older, Mother didn't display much of the spirit she had shown throughout my boyhood. My children remember her as nice but serious. She could be funny, though. When Rodora and I moved our family from Hibbing to Sioux Falls, Mother enjoyed visiting us because, as she put it, she could see. Her view wasn't blocked by thick stands of trees!

If my parents weren't content in their relationship, they never showed it to my brother and me. I had a boyhood in which I felt loved, one in which I had the security of being part of a family whose parents at least presented a united front.

A Scout is...loyal and courteous

Chapter 2

EXPLORING THE NEIGHBORHOOD AND PEDDLING PAPERS

When I was a boy, my world consisted of two square blocks. We lived at 610 4th Avenue, in a house that was about 24 feet wide with three rooms on the first floor and a glassed-in front porch. The bedrooms were on the second floor.

Neighborhood children were my playmates, and their mothers looked after all of us. In particular, Gladys Enzman took care of Bob and me, and Mother took care of the Enzman boys, Art and Don. No one called him Art, however. That was his father's name and reserved for him. To us, the younger Art was Skeezix, because he had been born the same year that the character Skeezix first appeared in the cartoon strip "Gasoline Alley."

Mr. Enzman, his brother, my grandfather and my dad would play the card game pitch often, and when I was five or six I used to sit on Dad's lap and watch him play. That's how I learned the game of pitch. I play it to this day and thanks to Dad's teaching, I often make my coffee money. He was a good pitch player, and so am I.

We children roamed the neighborhood, never getting into serious trouble but taking part in games such as tin can alley, naturally played in an alley, and anti-anti-high-over, played over the neighbor's garage right behind our house. Our sports weren't structured the way they are today: no coaches or referees or uniforms and no belligerent parents on the sidelines. We'd play baseball and football with whoever was around, and whoever had equipment would share it. If you tried to run home and another boy said "You're out!," then you were out, no arguments. We depended on each other to play fair.

International Falls was a mix of ethnic groups, but I'm not aware of any conflicts. If there were any, it wasn't between us kids. It would have been a grown-up thing. There probably was some level of unease between the Catholics and the Protestants but again not with the children. Discrimination is something that adults teach children; they don't come by it on their own.

Two blocks from home was the ice house. We played down there in the summertime. It contained huge chunks of ice that men cut from the lake in the winter and packed with sawdust to be stored all summer. The iceman would come in a horse-drawn buggy, and he would chip the ice to fit the size of each family's ice box. We kids would be right there at the back of the wagon, eating the chips as he carved the ice.

The milkman was another frequent visitor to the house, coming from the south end of International Falls. It was raw milk, never pasteurized in those days. In fact, the first time I had pasteurized milk was when we went to visit my Aunt Esther in St. Paul in the 1930s. I made a face: What was this stuff?

A man named Gustafson had a construction yard and building nearby; we treated his equipment as our own personal playground. The neighborhood also included a Finnish bath, which the Finns on Friday and Saturday would visit after a hard week working in the mills. Charlie Smith's blacksmith shop was down the alley from the Finnish bath. He welcomed visiting children, never chasing us away, so it was fun to go there.

In the evening, we would gather 'round to listen to the radio. Our favorites were shows such as "Inner Sanctum" and "The Lone Ranger" and listening to world heavyweight boxing champion Joe Louis fight his opponents.

But it wasn't all play time. My first job came when I was six years old. My father and I were playing with an electric train, which I still have, when I asked him for a dime to go to the motion pictures. A dime may not sound like much now, but the Depression already had started. My father probably was earning twenty-five cents an hour, working ten-hour days.

After hearing my request, Dad suggested that it was time I earned my own entertainment money. At age six, about the only option open to me was to peddle papers, selling them door to door. My first job led to an early lesson, one I've never forgotten.

I began selling the Minneapolis Sunday Tribune in the winter. Because I was just starting, I didn't have a cloth bag to hold the papers. Instead, I took three papers and put them on my sled, intending to sell them door to door. But I'd barely gotten started when a gust of wind came up and blew all three papers off the sled. Crying, I headed home.

When I got there, however, my dad said, "Come on, let's go out and look for those papers." We went back to that neighborhood, picked up the pages that were plastered against fences, trees and bushes and reassembled them, although I'm sure there were some missing. And I went back out and sold all three papers.

That's when I learned that no matter what adversity faces you, you need to solve the problem. And I AM a problem-solver. I've said for years that I'm not in the hardware business, I'm in the problem-solving business. People come through the store door, and they have a problem. Our job is to solve it for them.

Sometimes they don't even have to walk in the door. A snowstorm smothered South Dakota on Christmas Eve and Christmas Day 2009. This excerpt from a story that ran in the December 30, 2009, Argus Leader demonstrates how well my son Kevin learned to be a problem-solver:

> There is no good time for a sewer backup. But Christmas Day, with family visiting during a record-setting blizzard, is an especially bad time.
>
> With six adults and five children unable to flush a toilet, Brad and Tammi Stangohr called every plumber they could find.

"Everybody said there's no way we can get out. The weather was too bad," said Tammi Stangohr, who lives between Sioux Falls and Brandon.

Seeing no other option, they looked up the home phone number for Kevin Nyberg and begged him to open one of his Ace Hardware stores so they could rent a sewer snake and make the repair themselves. A half-hour later, the plumbing tool in hand, Christmas was saved.

"He didn't hesitate a bit," Stangohr said. "He was just extremely helpful."

Nyberg said he was expecting at least one such Christmas phone call.

"That's what we do. We're there to help. It doesn't bother me," he said. "That's what built the business."

Being a problem-solver also applies to one's personal life. I don't believe in letting a problem sit unresolved, festering until it worsens. I don't know how many times I said this to my son, Kevin, or to store employees, "If you've got a problem, solve it! Why keep being pestered by it? Put your mind to solving the cotton-picking problem."

I continued to sell newspapers on Sundays for about six years, making about two cents per paper. Eventually I built up regular customers for my route. When I was about 12 years old, I took on two established paper routes, delivering the International Falls Daily Journal in the evening and the Duluth News-Tribune in the morning. My first boss was a man named Bo McCormick.

Being *involved* with a newspaper route also took me out of my usual *environment*, offering *exposure* to other areas, through trips offered to contest winners for the Duluth Herald and News Tribune. Those trips and going to Tennessee to meet Mother's relatives were the only times I left Minnesota. For example, in 1941 when I was 15, 41 of us took a trip to Chicago. We traveled overnight by train, having a breakfast of cooked or dry cereals, eggs cooked any way we wanted them and rolls (I still have the mimeographed menu). We toured the Swift Packing Plant and the Field Museum and ate in Chinatown. The next day, we toured the Chicago Municipal Airport, and at 2:00

p.m. we were seated at Wrigley Field, ready to cheer on the Chicago Cubs vs. the Pittsburgh Pirates. I have the scorecard from that game, too. The scorecard cost ten cents and it shows that bleacher seats were fifty-five cents and a box seat went for $1.65. I didn't keep score, though, so I don't know who won the game!

Success in another sales drive sent me on a trip to Minneapolis to see the University of Golden Gophers football team play the University of Nebraska Cornhuskers.

I kept those paper routes until I was 16 and started working in the hardware store. I probably would have kept the routes even longer because I was making good money, about as much as some grown men were earning. But one day the hardware store owner, Rudy Erickson, said to me, "Roy, you can't be a slave to two masters." He was telling me I had a choice to make.

My Social Security card was issued April 25, 1938. The federal program itself only started in 1935; I think I probably had to get a card that young because the Minnesota & Ontario Paper Company owned the Daily Journal, and it required all its employees to have a Social Security number. The back of the card warns sternly "Keep a record of this number as you might lose the card."and you were told not to tell your number to anyone.

I laugh now when I think how OSHA officials would react to my early work. The Daily Journal printing press was on the first floor. The press's hot metal arms would come down and go up in a quick rhythm; you had to reach in when the arm was going up, pull out the freshly printed newspaper and then fold it.

I found my Sunday customers by going door to door, asking people if they wanted to buy a paper. The daily routes were already established. One paper route took me to the Forest Inn, built to house mill employees who were single men. That area had about 25 bars, and the town itself had three churches. Okay, that might be a slight exaggeration. But it was an interesting part of town. My route was on the north side of 3rd Street, International Falls' main street, running from 2nd to 6th Avenue. Second Street was the area with the most fascinating residents.

My route included four girls-of-the-night houses. And, yes, even at that age I knew what they were. I specifically was told never to collect in the morning but to wait until about suppertime, when the girls would be awake and ready for the evening's business. I knew the female residents by name. Some of the girls were about the only black people in our town. A madam lived nearby in a house with her girls; several other brothels were located in apartments. The madam was disfigured by venereal disease, or so the story went. At one point, long after I'd stopped delivering papers, she became ill and needed to be hospitalized. Mother already was in the hospital for some reason, and the nurse asked her if she would share her two-bed room with the madam since the hospital had no other beds available. My mother was a gracious lady, and she agreed.

I also peddled papers to the Busy Bee, a bar on 4th Avenue. It was half a block away from the mill entrance. I seldom met my dad after work, but one swelteringly hot day in July I waited for him at the gate. We were walking by the Busy Bee when Dad's helper asked him to stop for a drink. I remember Dad hesitated, looking down at me. I'm sure he didn't want to take me into the bar while he had a drink, but it had been a long, hot day, and he was thirsty.

So we went inside. I didn't have anything to drink, of course, but we both stood at the bar, a foot on the brass rail. My father must have felt a bit guilty because he said to me, "Son, there's nothing wrong with drink as long as you're man enough to know when to quit." That made quite an impression on me, and I have followed his advice – with one or two exceptions.

My mother's younger sisters also played an important role in my childhood. They were only six and eight years older than I was, and they were fond of me. To them it was like having a baby brother. When I was 14, Florence, the older of the two, gave me a phonograph record. I remember going upstairs and sitting on my bed and playing that song all day long. Called "Elmer's Tune," it became a No. 1 hit for Glenn Miller in 1941. The first verse goes "Why are the stars always winkin' and blinkin' above? It's not the season – the reason is plain as the moon – It's just Elmer's Tune."

A sulfur odor from the mills hung over International Falls. When the smokestacks were made taller, and winds blew from the west and northwest, we could smell the sulfur at our lake cabin. Sometimes Dad would give people a tour of the mill, and we'd go along. They had a porthole in one furnace wall that you could walk up to and feel a cool draft, much more pleasant than the heat coming from the burners. But you also could smell the sulfur, and it would clear your lungs.

International Falls is right across the border from Fort Francis, Canada, and it was a five-mile span from the Canadian shore to our beach. When I was a boy, it was common just to walk across the bridge to go into Canada. If you drove or walked, you had to pay a toll of a nickel or a dime. You had to pass through Canadian customs on your way north and U.S. customs upon your return, but that was no big deal.

Mother belonged to clubs that met in Fort Francis, and as I grew older, I would attend dances in Fort Francis with my friends. It's worth noting that all five of my closest boyhood friends married Canadian girls. I know they were love matches, but there also was something alluring for the girl about becoming an American citizen.

Growing up in International Falls meant bracing yourself for long, bitterly cold winters. But because we grew up with it, because it was all you knew, we really didn't think it was all that bad. I've often said I'd take a –30° day in International Falls, with its dry air and stillness, than a 0° day in Sioux Falls with higher humidity and strong winds. The dampness makes you feel colder.

You learned as children to wind a scarf over your face, to put a hat on your head to keep your body heat in, and to wear overshoes on your feet to keep the cold away whenever you went outside. Usually, on school days, we went home for lunch. There was no cafeteria in school and certainly no hot-lunch program. But if it was going to be 30° below zero at noon, we carried a cold lunch to school, eating it in the assembly room.

International Falls recorded a temperature reading of -40° in February 2008, a record. But our own thermometers often showed that temperatures had dipped as low as 50° below zero. I remember once standing in our glassed-in front porch, looking at the snow-covered streets which wouldn't be bare again until the spring thaw. I could hear something coming closer, going "Crunch, crunch, thud, thud. Crunch, crunch, thud, thud." Suddenly a group of Ukrainians came into view, beards frosted with ice formed by their breathing, walking to their jobs at the mill. They were wearing heavy coats, but every few steps – which crunched on the snow – they then would slap their chests with their hands to keep warm – thud, thud.

My father had a car called a Whippet. When the coldest stretch of winter began, he took the tires off, rims and all, and stored them in the basement. That meant we walked everywhere, or if we were young enough, we'd ride on a sled and our parents would pull us to our destination. I remember once my father put a harness on my uncle's dog, and he pulled our sled for us.

My mother would walk to Rogenrud's, a small neighborhood grocery store, just 1½ blocks away, and carry the food home. Several years later, a National Tea grocery store came to International Falls, opening right outside the mill. Mother shopped there sometimes because the prices were cheaper than the small Mom-and-Pop stores. But it bothered her because Rogenrud's always had extended us credit during the lean times.

Life was good if you were a boy in International Falls in the 1930s. But it was not all play and peddling papers. There also was school and, for me at least, Scouting.

A Scout is...obedient and thrifty

Chapter 3
SCOUTING, ACE AND WOMEN

Probably the two greatest influences on my life have been my parents and Scouting.

I didn't begin my *involvement* with Cub Scouts the way many young boys do today. Cub Scouts started nationally in 1930, and we didn't have that option yet. Instead, I was 13 years old when I joined the Boy Scouts in 1939. My boyhood pal and neighbor Don Enzman and I decided, for some reason or another, we wanted to become Scouts. We took it seriously, and we would chastise each other whenever we violated the Scout laws. Don left Scouting after a short time, but I stuck with it.

Becoming a Boy Scout is a decision I've never regretted. It has been 70 years since I was required to memorize it, but to this day I can recite the Boy Scout oath in one breath: "On my honor I will do my best to do my duty to God and my country and to obey the Scout Law; to help other people at all times; to keep myself physically strong, mentally awake, and morally straight." I also can recite the Scout Law: trustworthy, loyal, helpful, friendly, courteous, kind, obedient, cheerful, thrifty, brave, clean and reverent.

Becoming a Scout provided me with both a healthy, wholesome *environment* and an *exposure* to numerous activities. I eventually became an Eagle Scout, and to do so, I had to earn 21 merit badges. That's 21 areas of *involvement* I was able to explore. Some were required; others were areas that I just wanted to learn more about. But either way, you were *exposed* to a lot of activities, you became proficient in them, and you remember them for life. To this day, there are things that I do that I first learned seven decades ago.

My troop, Troop 147, was sponsored by the International Falls Junior Chamber of Commerce, an organization that later became known as the Jaycees. Eventually, I became an assistant troop leader, ascending from treasurer and assistant patrol leader. In the summer of 1944, after I had graduated from high school, I was a junior officer at Black Point Camp near International Falls. Early *exposure* to leadership would pave the way for my activities as an adult.

When I think about Scouting, I remember all the fun we Scouts had. In International Falls on the Fourth of July, a parade would wind down the city streets. We Scouts would serve food, selling hamburgers or hot dogs or pop to the people who attended. Trygve Anderson was my scout master for many years. He was an industrial arts teacher, and I have no doubt that he was the one who actually built our refreshment stand. We boys just "helped."

I have a newspaper clipping from the International Falls Daily Journal that shows me with five other Scouts. We had distributed throughout the city defense savings posters, urging people to help with the war effort by buying savings bonds, following the Boy Scout creed of showing patriotism and providing community service.

A Scout camp was less than a mile to the northeast of my family's cabin, located on the same peninsula at Rainy Lake. All I had to do was walk through the woods, and I'd be at the Scout camp. I spent every summer from the age of 8 to 17 at the lake and in the woods, either at our own place or the Scout camp.

The Scout camp had one building on the grounds in those days. We slept in tents except for one time when a storm was coming through the area, and we gathered in the lone building. I learned how to canoe in Scouting. Not many of my friends had boats with outboard motors – only the children of the men who made the most money at the mills.

In International Falls, Nordahl Olson was the man recognized unofficially as "Mr. Scout." He was a bachelor and devoted to Scouting. One night, both Mr. Olson and I were being initiated into the Order of the Arrow. We were supposed to spend the night outdoors, but it was starting to rain, and the mosquitoes were particularly bad. I'm just glad I was teamed up with Mr. Olson because he said, "I'm not taking this. We're going inside." And we did.

I stayed involved with Scouting after I became an adult. After I returned from World War II, I helped start a Boy Scout troop in Minneapolis, but I didn't have enough time to devote to that. I also was a charter member when Our Savior's Lutheran Church Men started a Boy Scout troop in Sioux Falls on February 28, 1959. We had 27 boys register to be part of that troop.

I officially became an Eagle Scout in August 1944. I had completed the requirements earlier, but the Eagle Scout ceremony took place only a couple times a year. As it turned out, I received my Eagle award on the day before I entered the Air Force. I was heading down to Fort Snelling in Minneapolis, and I stopped in Hibbing, Minnesota, where Judge Chris Holm awarded me my Eagle rank. My parents and my brother, Bob, were there for the ceremony.

Two of my three Scoutmasters, including Trygve Anderson, already had entered the armed forces. The story in the Daily Journal says that my plans for the future "include work in Scouting and he is considering the possibility of making it his life's profession." Well, that's what the story says, but as important as Scouting was to me, I already knew that someday I wanted my own hardware store.

I had started at the hardware store when I was 16, at the beginning of my junior year in high school. To this day, I'm not sure who recommended me for the job. It could have been my Scoutmaster or maybe the typing teacher.

Now, keep in mind, World War II was underway, and many men already had gone into the service. Rudy Erickson, who owned Erickson Hardware, couldn't spend much time at his hardware store. He supervised the wartime rationing center in International Falls and also had other responsibilities. During World War II, items such as tires, gasoline, butter, sugar and coffee were rationed. You couldn't just walk into a store and buy as much of those items as you wanted to, even if you had the money. Rudy's position carried a lot of responsibility with it.

He relied on a woman named Ida Gilsoul to manage the store for him and had four other female employees. But he also needed someone with a strong back. That's where I came in.

I weighed only 126 pounds when I entered the service, so as a high school junior, I weighed even less. Nevertheless, the first job I had to do every day after school was carry at least four or five one-hundred-pound round nail kegs up a flight of stairs and empty them into the nail bin. There were no glue guns or staple guns at that time. Everything was nailed or screwed so a hardware store like ours went through a lot of nails. We used ball peen hammers to open the nail kegs. I wish I had some of those kegs today.

I also had to hammer stovepipe that was 3 to 11 inches in diameter. Today when you assemble such pipe, it has a joint that self-locks. But in the 1940s, you had to put the galvanized pipes between your legs, crunch them together, lay them on an anvil, and hammer the seam to seal the joint. It was tough work, particularly because my hands are not particularly large.

Another early job was washing the store's exterior windows once a week. Rudy himself taught me how to do that, and I became the best window-washer there was. I swept the floors with an oil-based compound, and when freight came in, I would open up the metal door on the sidewalk outside and slide the merchandise down a chute into the basement. Also, I checked merchandise in, verified the quantities, and then priced it.

Erickson Hardware belonged to the Ace Hardware chain, and I learned the "Ace-ified" way of doing things. In fact, I taught those procedures to a man to whom I had once sold newspapers on my daily route. Harvey Remer had been employed at the Woolworth's in International Falls before he moved to Iowa and became a regional manager for the dime store chain. But he returned to International Falls and went into the hardware store business with Rudy Erickson, and they opened a store in Hibbing, about 100 miles away.

For five or six months, I taught Mr. Remer the Ace program, showing him the invoices and how to check in the merchandise. We even built display racks in the basement. Several years later, he became my boss. How many people do you suppose can say they trained their future boss when they were only 17?

The irony is, I was supposed to go to Hibbing and help them open up a new store. I was scheduled to move there in August 1944. It was a big deal for me, a recent high school graduate. I would have stayed in a hotel for several months. But my Army call came about the time I was supposed to leave, so it was decided there was no purpose in sending me down. But that wouldn't be my last connection with the Ace Hardware store in Hibbing.

The hardware store in International Falls was affected by the war, just as everything was. Just before I started, the basement flooded, and all the appliances that Rudy Erickson had stockpiled to get him through the war were ruined. I helped haul them out of the basement and to the dump.

Only the tops and bottoms of paint cans were made of metal. The cylinder itself was of a heavy cardboard. I remember the paint cans clearly because of a memory that involves the most famous man to come out of International Falls, Bronko Nagurski. His folks ran a neighborhood grocery store, only about half a block from where I lived. It was covered in green shingles, like the shingles you put on the roof.

Bronko was of Polish-Ukrainian descent. He was born in Canada, but his folks moved to International Falls when he was a boy. He played professional football for the Chicago Bears from 1930 to 1937 and also became a professional wrestler during that time. He was a three-time world heavyweight champion. In 1943, he returned to the Bears for one season, then went out to California for a year before returning to wrestling. Rodora and I saw Bronko wrestle several times before we were married. He later purchased a service station in International Falls.

Bronko was a big man for the time, standing six feet, two inches. He came into the store one day, accompanied by his five-year-old son. He bought five one-gallon cans of paint, and when he left he picked up his son and the five gallon paint cans and walked off. He had property on Rainy Lake, too, and when he had a boulder on his property that needed to be moved, he just rolled it away. I actually saw him do this.

I enjoyed my work at the hardware store. I used to leave school an hour early, at two o'clock, and head straight to work. Okay, sometimes I would stop at the drugstore first and buy a ten-cent malt.

The women who worked at the hardware store had a big influence on me, and I emulated their manner with the customers. It was the beginning of a lifetime of working with women and valuing what they have to teach me. They were always courteous and helpful, and I modeled myself after them. I did whatever was asked of me, and I didn't leave things half done.

But despite my liking for the work, and the lessons I was learning about being a boss from Ida Gilsoul, during my senior year of high school I decided I was going to quit the hardware store. With so many men off to war, good workers were scarce. The Minnesota & Ontario Paper Mill was asking high school boys and girls who were seniors to come work there three days a week, from 3:00 to 9:00 p.m. That was 18 hours work, and the mill paid $250 a month.

At the hardware store, I was working from 2:00 to 6:00 p.m. weekdays and all day Saturday. And my paycheck was only $25 a month! So I gave Ida my notice, and she accepted it.

Rudy Erickson was hardly there in the daytime, busy as he was with his other duties. But after he heard I was quitting, he came up to me when I was carrying a nail keg upstairs. I'll never forget what he said to me. "I can guarantee you, you're going to go over to the mill and make $250 a month," he said. "Then you're going to go in the service, and you're going to come home, and you're going to remember that good money. You'll probably end up pushing a machine, pushing a machine for the rest of your life." He told me to go home, think it over, and tell Ida Gilsoul my decision the next day. Then he added, "And there won't be a raise."

I thought about what he said overnight, and the next day I came in and said, "I'll stay."

Why did I do that? Why did I stay? The prospect of making ten times more money with fewer hours was certainly enticing.

But I came up with several reasons for staying at the hardware store: 1) I was being given a man's job with a man's responsibility while I was only a teenager. 2) I already was looking toward the future, one that didn't involve "pushing a machine" for 40 years. 3) I had developed a passion for the hardware business.

And, finally, because there was a war on.

A Scout is...trustworthy and helpful

Chapter 4

SCHOOL DAYS AND TEEN ACTIVITIES

At the age of five, I marched through the doors of the Alexander Baker Elementary School, named after the man who first built a log cabin at what became International Falls. School became the *environment* where I would spend the most time until my graduation in 1944, a place where I became *involved* with others and *exposed* to a variety of classes.

International Falls had two school buildings in the early 1930s. Elementary pupils attended Alexander Baker. Junior high students, freshmen, sophomores, juniors and seniors attended Falls High School. About the time I reached the middle grades, the E.W. Backus Junior High School opened. It was named after an early president of the Minnesota & Ontario Paper Company, the city's largest business and employer.

The first school in International Falls had been started in 1896, but no high school program began until the fall of 1909. A combination elementary-high school was opened in 1914. Alexander Baker Elementary and Backus Junior High School both were three-story buildings, while the high school stood two stories tall. The high school building, opened in 1924, two years before I was born, later was torn down, but the elementary and junior high buildings still stand, preserved by International Falls residents who prize history.

Several years ago, I played a role in the buildings' continued existence, suggesting to preservationists that former schoolrooms be set aside for civic clubs and others to use in storing and displaying records and memorabilia. Lo and behold, organizers picked up on some of that, and today various rooms are being used for displays.

I had some great teachers in International Falls, although not all of my "teachers" were in the classroom. In 2000, I made a contribution to the Falls Education Foundation in memory of Bo McCormick, Trygve Anderson, Wayne Judy, Agnes Pirkl and Rudy Erickson. Only Wayne Judy and Agnes Pirkl were my teachers in the traditional sense: Mr. Judy taught industrial arts at the junior high school, and Miss Pirkl led the accounting classes at Falls High School. Bo McCormick was my first boss when I became a newsboy, Trygve Anderson was a scoutmaster, and Rudy Erickson owned the hardware store where I began working at age 16. Mr. McCormick hired me when I was 15. I already knew him through my paper route. He was a magazine distributor, and he hired me to distribute the magazines to stores and collect the ones that didn't sell and tear off the covers so he could return them for credit.

Yes, some of my classroom teachers were terrific, but I'm afraid I wasn't an outstanding student. I have all my report cards, and I would label myself a solid C student. Part of the problem was during the Depression, very few of us thought we would go on to a profession such as doctor or lawyer. We knew the money for college just wasn't there.

I did better in non-scholastic areas. In first grade, I was given an A in courtesy and in being cheerful and keeping my temper, "even when things go wrong." I received B's in trustworthiness, industry (or "work spirit"), initiative and thrift, and a C in courage, which was defined as attacking difficult tasks bravely.

But by the time I entered seventh grade, it is apparent from my report cards that studying was not something that took up a lot of my time. Grades included a D in English, C's in general science and arithmetic, a C+ in social studies, a B- in industrial arts, and a B in art. Pre-printed on the report card was an ominous statement: "The 'D' student is headed for failure." My junior year was better: C's in English and American history, B's in industrial arts, typing, band and orchestra, and a D in chemistry. My senior year I had the best grades ever: A's in orchestra and band, a B in bookkeeping, and C's in English, social science and industrial arts.

Obviously, you don't need to earn straight A's to succeed in business, at least not in the climate of 65 years ago. But I'm not sure why I didn't do better in school. I know I didn't receive any help at home from my parents. My Swedish-immigrant father would sit in a chair and read the newspaper every night. I was proud of the fact he didn't speak with a Swedish accent. But to this day, I'm not sure he could actually write in English. Certainly, I could not expect much help from him. And my mother, an intelligent woman, had too much to do around the house in that age before today's labor-saving appliances to sit at the kitchen table and help my brother and me with our homework.

Also, from the age of six, I had begun to earn my own income with the newspaper route, and other jobs followed. School was not always a priority.

I know why I got that D in chemistry: I did not like that teacher! I had him for biology, too. But our relationship had started when I was in fifth grade. During the Depression, I began taking violin lessons. My family had a half-size violin, a beautiful one, a copy of a Stradivarius that my granddaughter Camryn uses today in grade school. It had been in the family for years. Fredrick Sands was the part-time music instructor and a full-time science teacher at the high school. There was no music store in International Falls so I'm guessing he also sold instruments on the side to make a little extra money.

Well, he ridiculed me for using a half-size violin to the point where it made me so mad that I just quit. I think he thought he could embarrass me into buying a full-size violin from him. But I didn't. And when I got to high school, I still was smarting from that *experience.* When I had him in a science class, I just absolutely would not work for that man!

I had intended to take physics, but Mr. Sands also taught that class so I never did. Physics would have been a great asset in some of the problem-solving you do at a hardware store, and I used to blame Mr. Sands. But someone pointed out a few years ago, "Roy, look at what that guy did. He made you divert from where you were thinking you wanted to be" – at that time I vaguely dreamed of architecture – "to commerce." It's true. He helped push me into bookkeeping, which was so unusual for a boy at that time that all the other students in that class were girls. I guess I am grateful to him – now.

But despite giving up the violin, I retained a love for music and played drums in the school band. I used to carry the marimba to and from school. At that time we were living in a house Dad had moved in from Lake Kabetogama to 9th Street and 9th Avenue, six blocks from the school. It was a 2½-octave marimba, so it was unwieldy and heavy.

My band instructor was a man who also eventually landed in South Dakota: Arne B. Larson, founder of the National Museum of Music in Vermillion. I remember him telling me, "Nyberg, you're always off beat."

I never played high school athletics, in part, I suppose, because I was a runt. Truly: I entered the service in 1944 weighing only 126 pounds. In junior high gym class, whenever we chose sides, I was the last one picked. But it wasn't unusual not to play sports; it was the Depression, and only the really good athletes took part. But that may be why I am so distressed at today's emphasis on athletics in school. I think much of that focus should be on academics. I said this often to my son, Kevin, when he was interested in playing sports in high school and also to my grandson, Erik: "You can't play football when you're 40." Athletics are great. But they take a toll on your body, and contact sports aren't something you can do your whole life, like hunting and golf.

An interest in music drew many of my friends together. Classmate Phil Agnew formed a band. It got me into trouble once. It was Labor Day 1943. Now, in International Falls, with the union and the mills, Labor Day was a big celebration. There was always a parade, led by a six foot, nine inch man who would make himself even taller with shoes soled with cleats and carry a Paul Bunyan-size ax. After the parade, a German band would travel from bar to bar, with the bartenders giving them all the beer they wanted just to coax the musicians into staying longer and keeping the customers entertained.

In 1943, the start of my senior year of high school, it rained "cats and dogs," an all-day rain. The parade was canceled. Phil, Jim Preece, who later became a circuit judge, Bob Ottenger and I decided to make the bar circuit, playing in place of the musicians who had gone to war. I carried my cymbals around to the bars.

Even though we were 17, the bartenders carried on the tradition of giving us free beer. After a few too many, I ended up at Jimmie's, a cafe and confectionery run by a Greek family, the Pagedas. My kid brother, Bob, saw me and reported it to our folks. I had my head on the table, when there's a tap on my shoulder. I look up, and there's my dad. Remember, he had told me several years earlier, "Son, there's nothing wrong with drink as long as you're man enough to know when to quit." On this day, I had forgotten his wise counsel.

He said, "Let's go, Roy. Let's go home. Where's the car?" We went outside to our black 1933 Chevrolet, and I head toward the passenger side. Dad goes, "Un-uh, get over there and drive." He's punishing me all the way. I get us home safely and literally crawl up the stairs to my bedroom, I'm that drunk. And it's only noon. But after sleeping the afternoon away, I sobered up and was ready to go to the dance being held that night.

I took part in other school activities. For several years I was captain of the school patrol, so I was allowed to leave school early to make sure the other guards all were in place!

Outside of school, in my free time, it was a great life. One memorable moment came when I was 12 years old, and I was given a bike. It came from a family friend, Ole Swanson, who had come over from Sweden. He was a bachelor, and my brother and I considered him another uncle. One day Mother called to me, and when I went to the back door, Ole was standing there with a brand-new bicycle. He had bought it with his bonus from serving in World War I. That was my first bike. If there is one regret I have, it is that I missed "Uncle" Ole's funeral 25 years later, probably because I was busy at the time with expanding my hardware store. I let work come before my family.

I loved dancing and going to dances. In the yearbook that came out my senior year, one prediction was that I would become a dancing teacher, in the style of Arthur Murray, who had founded a chain of dance studios that still bear his name and also taught dance steps through a mail-order course.

The cold winters of International Falls, billed as the Icebox of the Nation, didn't stop us from having fun.

The city would plow a four-lane highway on Rainy Lake's Black Bay for people to just drive their cars on. Seriously. With a constant string of temperatures that hit 30° below zero, the ice probably was three feet thick. It was just like a racetrack. On the way out, we did maneuvers that I can describe best as water-skiing on ice. We would take a rope and tie it behind the car, and someone would balance on skis and hold onto the rope. We'd be down in the ditch, and along comes someone's mailbox, and we had to flip the tow rope over that mailbox to stay in the ditch. Then we'd get out to Black Bay, and the snow probably was three feet deep because of the winds blowing it into the bay. You're going 60 miles an hour behind these cars, and momentum would carry you to the side so you could see the car's driver!

We had family in International Falls and nearby. One of my mother's sisters, Mary, lived in Loman, about 20 miles to the west. She was married to a logger who also raised strawberries commercially. I went out to visit one weekend. Uncle Oscar was bringing me back in his red pickup truck. In the back was a Christmas tree we had cut down for Mother and Dad. It was Mother's birthday that day.

The two of us were in that red pickup truck, and the snow just was coming down softly, in perfect, fluffy flakes. Few vehicles had been on the road, so we were making our own tracks. It was just a beautiful, snowy day. I can remember walking into our back porch, and Mom saying, "The Japs bombed Pearl Harbor." Like so many other people did that day, Uncle Oscar and I asked, "Where the heck is Pearl Harbor?" He headed home, and we glued ourselves to the radio for the rest of the night.

It was December 7, 1941. Everything was about to change.

A Scout is…friendly and cheerful

Chapter 5

WORLD EVENTS CHANGE MY LIFE

There is no question of the impact the United States entering into World War II had on my generation.

It changed the *environment* in which we lived, increased our *exposure* to and awareness of what was happening on the world stage, and altered our *involvement* in everyday life.

I never would have started working in a hardware store at age 16 if the owner hadn't been short of manpower because of the war. I never would have been the only male working there, giving myself an early appreciation of the capabilities of women in an era when most of us saw females only as mothers or teachers.

We boys spent our high school years watching as young men slightly older than we were registered for the draft. One draft registration took place June 30, 1942, for men 18 to 20 years of age, quickly followed by one December 10th through 31st of that same year. We knew that when we turned 18, even if we were still in high school, if we were physically able we would be drafted at once into the military. My high school graduating class had 85 members. It would have been larger, but some boys couldn't wait and voluntarily enlisted in the service.

My high school yearbook with its mimeographed pages on inexpensive paper bears little resemblance to the nicely bound volumes with color photos that today's graduates have as remembrances. Instead, it is 49 mimeographed pages held together with staples. After the yearbook's optimistic dedication ("The world is ours!"), the foreword notes, "The Falls High Seniors of 1943 and 1944 have been rather unfortunate in having to go through their high school days under restrictions due to wartime conditions. However, this did not undermine their spirit and versatility."

My class ring has a gold veneer with a silver-metal interior. The school district offered a traditional junior-senior prom in 1942 but canceled in 1943 as a cost-saving measure. It was held again in 1944 so the classes of 1944 and 1945 would have at least one prom to remember.

We boys, at least, used our impending enlistment to persuade our parents to let us do things that otherwise would have been forbidden. On Labor Day 1943, when I had come home intoxicated at noon, Mother wanted to punish me by refusing to let me attend that night's dance. But I wheedled and pleaded until she gave her permission, reminding her that next year I probably would be off fighting in the war and I needed to have fun while I could.

Within two years, my *involvement* in World War II was a sure thing. In November 1943, I enlisted in the U.S. Army Air Forces. That meant two things: It was guaranteed that I would serve in that branch of the military, and I knew I would be able to finish my senior year at Falls High School.

A Scout is…brave and clean

Chapter 6
ARMY LIFE BEGINS

On November 8, 1943, when I enlisted in the Army Air Forces, as it then was called, I had aspirations of being a pilot. That goal gave me the designation of air cadet. For the rest of my senior year in high school, I could use the initials "A/C" to identify myself and my intentions. The Army Air Forces just had been established in 1941, so we generally called it by its old name, the Army Air Corps.

What remained unknown was when I would enter the Air Corps. I graduated from Falls High School on May 18, 1944, not knowing exactly when I would be needed so I continued to work at the hardware store.

But in August, just as I prepared to leave for Hibbing to help open the new hardware store that was the partnership of Rudy Erickson and Harvey Remer, I learned that the Air Corps was summoning me. I was ordered to report to Fort Snelling in the Twin Cities on August 23, 1944, and told I would take basic training at Amarillo Army Air Field in Texas.

Before my departure, my co-workers at Erickson's Hardware threw a party, combing my farewell with another employee's birthday. Ida Gilsoul hosted the party in her home on a Tuesday evening. The five women I'd been working with for months all signed a greeting card.

My parents and younger brother accompanied me to St. Paul, and they stayed with my Aunt Esther, Dad's sister. We posed for a picture, the four of us in a row. My father is wearing a white shirt and tie; my mother's hair is in carefully arranged curls. My face has the biggest smile, and I'm wearing the shirt and tie from my new uniform. My parents must have wondered if they'd ever have their family together again. I carried a wallet-sized photo with me all through the service. I still have it although Bob's face is a little worn and faded since he is on the end.

My departure for the Army Air Corps ended any chance Bob and I had to become close as boys. Remember, I was 4½ years older than Bob, so he was just 13 when I left home. The age difference meant we hadn't played together much. I never wanted my little brother hanging around when I had my own friends.

But I wasn't completely uncaring. After I left for the service, I would send him models of trucks, tanks and such for him to assemble. Bob still has part of a T-shirt I sent him that says, "My brother is in the Air Force at Amarillo Air Base."

I remember once when I was home on furlough, Bob said, "Roy, let's go down to the basement." We walked downstairs, and that kid had devised a mock anti-aircraft gun out of cardboard. He could sit on it, it had a barrel, and it would revolve. He made it out of the cardboard cores that factories wrap linoleum around. A few years later, he began studying drafting at Dunwoody Institute in Minneapolis, but he evidently had a talent from the very beginning.

I wasn't at Fort Snelling long before I left for Amarillo and 90 days of basic training. I also learned fairly soon that I was not going to be a pilot. The doctors examined my eyes and rejected me for flying. I never got a clear explanation of what was wrong, but the doctors turned out to be right. Labor Day weekend of 1954, Rodora and I were driving from her folks' farm south of the Twin Cities back to our home in Hibbing, and the constant barrage of headlights coming south put a strain on my eyes. When we got home, I walked into our kitchen and for some reason closed my left eye. My right eye remained open, but I couldn't even see the clock on the wall. At an appointment at Mayo Clinic a few weeks later, I learned I had problems that couldn't be reversed. The vision worsened, and today I have no sight in my right eye. I get along okay, it just causes problems with hunting.

But the Air Corps could use me in other ways. And I don't recall being all that disappointed because I wasn't going to be a pilot. You did what you were told to do and rolled with the punches. I am sorry today that I didn't use my leftover time with the GI Bill of Rights to learn how to fly privately, however.

I did find one thing I could do for the Army right away. They needed a small band for Saturday parade inspections. They asked for volunteers, and about four of us did. So all the while I was in basic training, I never once had to have my rifle inspected because I was in the band. In fact, I directed it!

Maybe I should have volunteered more often. But I never was a brown-noser, and I knew the Army was not going to be my career. The only time I regretted not volunteering was when I was stationed in Italy, and a brand-new plane had its left wing blown off because someone wearing cleats on his shoes set off a spark while it was being refueled. The Army asked for volunteers to put the electrical radio back in shape. I was close to going home so I didn't volunteer. Turns out, if I had, I would have been flown home instead of facing a long ride on a ship!

I took a test in basic training to determine what I might be good at. I misunderstood one test and gave all the wrong answers, which kept me out of cryptography school. Had I passed and been trained to encrypt messages, I probably would have been sent behind the lines.

Instead, I ended up being assigned to aircraft radio mechanics school to learn how to repair radios. Two air bases near my home state of Minnesota offered both radio mechanics and radio operation: one in Sioux Falls, South Dakota, the other in Madison, Wisconsin.

My orders at one point were cut for the air base in Sioux Falls. But after I left Amarillo, I went to Scott Field in St. Louis, Missouri, and there I learned I would be going to Truax in Madison instead. Truax Field had been activated as an Army Air Base in June 1942 and wasn't deactivated as an active military base until 1968.

Several years ago, I visited with the late Sid Epstein, a businessman who came to Sioux Falls during his service in World War II as a quartermaster and never left. When I told him I originally had been assigned to Sioux Falls and didn't know why it had been changed, he reminded me that in late 1944, the war in the European theater was beginning to wind down. "We were packed, we were full," Sid said about the Sioux Falls air base at that period. They didn't have room for any more servicemen "so that's why your orders were relayed, and you went to Truax."

Before I left Texas, I was involved in one incident that had a lasting effect. In fact, I think it and a health issue a few months later delayed my training so long that it twice took me out of the rotation and delayed my being sent overseas while the war still was going on.

We were out in the desert one day on a maneuver called route step, when you can talk to each other and your lines don't have to be straight. The fellow ahead of me had his rifle slung not vertically but horizontally. Someone called out "Tarantula!" and stepped on the spider. The guy ahead of me turned around to talk to his buddy, directly behind me, and whacked me right across the mouth with his rifle. It hurt, but I didn't think much of it.

But by the time I reached Chanute, two air bases later, the teeth had abscessed badly. They had to be removed and replaced with a permanent gold bridge. The problem with my teeth required me to stay behind when the men I'd trained with in Amarillo moved on.

My time in Madison meant I was able to be with family at Christmas every year I was in the service. For Christmas 1944 I had a fifty-one-hour pass and met my folks in St. Paul. That was the first time we'd seen each other since August.

In February 1945 I made my first trip back to International Falls. It was written up in the International Falls Daily Journal, which reported that on a forty-hour pass, I took the train to Spooner, Wisconsin. My folks met me there and took me back to International Falls. We arrived home at 6:30 a.m., and by 2:30 p.m. I had to repeat the journey so I wouldn't be AWOL. (Actually, distance-wise, I already had been AWOL. My forty-hour pass contained distance restrictions. Spooner was supposed to be as far as I could travel.)

It was great to be home even for a little while. While I was away I had received letters from Ida Gilsoul and other women I'd worked with at the hardware store. Two young men had been hired in my absence. They fired one of them for being a lazy dud, and they said the other one didn't have any personality. They wished they had me back.

At Truax, I learned to be a radio mechanic. But I also picked up a part-time job off the base, loading and unloading freight cars at the Ray-O-Vac battery plant, as it was known until 1988 when the name changed to Rayovac. We had sold Ray-O-Vac batteries when I worked in the hardware store in International Falls.

I was stationed at Truax when V-E Day arrived May 8, 1945, signaling the end of the war in Europe. We weren't let off base, so you know those pictures of excited servicemen kissing every girl in sight? That wasn't me. I'm still irritated by that!

On August 15, 1945, World War II came to an end. I don't know if I'd be here today if it hadn't been for President Truman dropping atomic bombs on Hiroshima and Nagasaki. Probably not, because they were anticipating a million men not coming back after invading Japan, and I surely would have been sent to the Pacific theater.

I was just boarding the train to go from Rantoul, Illinois, to Boca Raton, Florida, on V-J Day so I did not get out in the street at all! The only thing we could do on the train was to holler "hip, hip, hooray!" at each other.

I knew the war's end did not mean an immediate discharge. The Army had a point system, and you received points for things such as length of service and overseas duty. You needed a certain number of points to be discharged. When you enlisted, it was understood you would remain until you had accumulated enough points toward a discharge.

From Truax I had gone to Chanute Air Force Base near Rantoul. I had other health problems besides my abscessed teeth. I needed to have my tonsils removed. Plus, I was assigned KP duty, so for hours we basically stood in water alongside a dishwasher we call the "China Clipper." Because of that, I developed a sinus infection and ended up in the hospital. The infection had so much pressure that my eyes squeezed shut for 30 days. The doctors did everything to try to relieve me of my sinus problems. They even inserted needles into my sinuses, but that didn't work. They then went in there and actually pounded into my skull and relieved the infection. Yes, that was as painful as it sounds.

I don't remember why I was sent to Chanute, probably to learn advanced radio skills before I went to Boca Raton. I even trained in radar, although I never used it much. From Boca Raton, I went to Selman Field in Monroe, Louisiana. I already had been told I would be going overseas. I spent Thanksgiving at Selman and still have the menu from the meal served that day: the traditional turkey, dressing and giblet gravy but with sweet potato pie rather than pumpkin.

It was while I was at Selman that the government introduced a program that stated if you would reenlist for a year, you would receive a $200 bonus and keep your rank. At that point, I'd already risen to corporal. I figured, well, wait a minute now. If they're going to send me overseas, they're not going to send me overseas just for a month or two and bring me home. Who knew how long I'd be gone? This way, I figured, I know that my tour of duty will be over in one year. So that's why I reenlisted November 12, 1945. I got home for Christmas 1945, and I think I got about a three-week vacation. The hometown paper reported, "Corporal Roy D. Nyberg is lucky enough to be home from Selman Field, Munroe (sic), Louisiana, to spend Christmas with his parents, Mr. and Mrs. Otto Nyberg, 610 4th Avenue. At Christmas dinner tomorrow the Nybergs will entertain Mrs. Nyberg's brother-in-law and sister, Mr and Mrs. Morris D. Stark; Mr. Nyberg's nephew, George Nyberg, recently discharged from the army, and his niece, Mrs. Bruno Lavigne and children, Sharon and Kenneth." Mrs. Lavigne was my cousin Elenore.

From home, I left for Greensboro, North Carolina, to prepare to head to Europe. If it hadn't been for a map and a string, I would have ended up in the Pacific. The policy at the time was, if your home was west of the Mississippi River, you were ordered to Salt Lake City; east of the Mississippi River, you went to Greensboro.

When I got to the desk, the sergeant seated there said, "International Falls? You're going to Salt Lake City." I said, "No, International Falls is east of the Mississippi. Look at a map. There's Bemidji. Bemidji is west. That's where the Mississippi starts, and it curves around. International Falls is east." "Well, it's so close it doesn't make a difference," was the answer I received. Most people would have let the matter drop right there. You didn't often talk back to a sergeant! But not me. I knew I was right and I wasn't afraid to prove it.

I put up enough of an argument that we finally went to a big map on the wall, ran a string from International Falls to North Carolina and from there to Salt Lake City. It was only a small difference, but I proved my point: International Falls was closer to North Carolina than Salt Lake City. The sarge gave in, and I headed off to the European theater.

To do my duty to God and my country

Chapter 7
TWO-AND-A-HALF CENTS AN HOUR, 24-7

I have a pay book from my years in the Army Air Forces that shows that, after a premium of $6.40 is taken out for insurance, Uncle Sam paid me $18.75 a month. That's $225 a year, but considering the Air Corps owned me, body and soul, twenty-four hours a day, seven days a week, it comes out to an hourly wage of two-and-a-half cents.

But, the military also provided room and board, clothing and a chance to travel. And in early 1946, the Air Force sent me to Italy. My departure date was February 8th. Before I left, I had spent a couple weeks in Greensboro, North Carolina, then was stationed at Camp Kilmer in New Brunswick, New Jersey, named after the poet who died in World War I. From there we were trucked over to the harbor in New York City, got on our Liberty ship, the New York University, and began the thirteen-day journey to Naples.

The date we were supposed to go overseas, I called my folks in International Falls. Dad asked, "How are you doing for money, Roy?" Despite earning only sixty cents a day, I could honestly say, "I'm all right. I've got about 500 bucks."

When I boarded the ship the next day, I was flat broke.

It's funny now but it wasn't funny then. I like to play cards, and I'm fairly decent at it. But I got myself into a craps game the night before we left for Italy, and I lost every cent I had. I didn't know a thing about playing craps, and some sharpies got to me.

Being broke was a problem because when you were being transferred, it took a couple months for your paycheck to catch up with you. We used military scrip money in the Post Exchanges, which were like retail stores. So the only money I had for weeks was what I got by selling my cigarette rations. Smoking wasn't a habit I'd picked up (I had tried it as a boy, buying the cigarettes from a neighborhood grocery store. I smoked one cigarette, and one was enough), so I didn't need the smokes provided by the government. But even then it wasn't American money because the cigarettes were sold on the black market, and I received Italian lira in exchange. I used the money to buy beautiful cameos. I had some made into rings, others into brooches. Some I gave to my aunts when I came home, and they have been returned to me over the years.

I could mail letters home without needing to buy stamps. But one time during this period of poverty, I had no stationery. So I went to the bathroom, purloined a roll of toilet paper, and wrote home to Mother on that, using a fountain pen. Actually, using toilet paper meant I had to improve my handwriting so it could be easily read, and some suggest even today that I should go back to using that as stationery.

The thirteen-day trip over meant no deck privileges because the weather and the sea together were so fierce. That January, ships were breaking up in the North Atlantic Ocean. Waves constantly beat against the bulkhead. When our ship would dip down into a rolling wave, it would rest at such an angle that the propellers hung in the air thrashing furiously, and the noise they made was ferocious. The whole ship would shake. A lot of the guys became seasick. I had the dry heaves for a couple of days but nothing serious. I took the rolling of the sea better than some of the others. I also was fortunate enough to have the top bunk, the fifth one up, alongside the bulkhead.

I still have a piece of paper with grids on it. We used those papers to play Battleship, a guessing game created before World War I, using PX's written in pencil to mark where we sunk our opponent's ships. We had to do something to pass the time because we did not see daylight for 13 days until we got to Gibraltar. Then we had a two-day break. We stopped at Casablanca, in North Africa, for refueling. There, the others tossed coins to the natives – I was broke, remember – who dove for them.

We disembarked at a camp that Italy's fascist leader Benito Mussolini had built to serve as a venue for the Olympics. That never happened, but it was a marvelous place with beautiful statues. The Americans had taken it over as a rest camp.

Naples had been bombed in World War II, and the headquarters at the Capodichino airfield was demolished in the raids. We lived in World War I sidewall tents for 11 months. The latrines were just holes in the floor of what remained of the headquarters building, but we did have a place for showers. We sent our clothes to the Army laundry or paid an Italian mother and daughter to wash and iron them for us.

We would have dances at a social club, and girls would be brought up on buses from Naples. They all had been carefully screened. I can remember one girl, good-looking as can be. She was a good dancer. Her left arm was scarred and burned, probably because of something that had happened in the war. You wondered what had occurred, but you didn't ask.

Despite the military's careful screening of our dance companions, I still have a base newspaper that warns about the rising rate of venereal disease among servicemen. At Capodichino, 25 new cases a month were being recorded. Because of that, the number of dances was reduced to two a week, and the story warns, "It may force Headquarters to tighten up on passes."

My discharge papers for my first stint in the service describe me as a radio mechanic. When I went to Italy, I was listed officially as a radar mechanic. But basically what I did was serve on the ground crew, working on the radio communications on the airplanes. We had been trained in radar because they were preparing us to serve in the Pacific theater, where they used radar more extensively than in Europe. Radar was one of the turning points in winning the war against Japan.

Although I was ground crew, that doesn't mean I didn't get up in the air. The squadron commander rotated every one of us, giving us the chance to make a few extra dollars with flying time. You got paid more for being in the air. I flew as a radio mechanic between Naples, Rome, Milan and Trieste.

Although World War II had ended, that didn't mean being stationed overseas still didn't have its dangers. I can remember Yugoslavia shooting down two planes from our base that ventured into its air space during the time I was stationed at Capodichino. One crew survived; the five men on the other plane all were killed.

It was a tense time, and the gruesomeness of the deaths made the situation worse. It was proved the crew had died when all or parts of four left feet were recovered from the wreckage. The Rome Daily American newspaper reported "sufficient human flesh had been found hanging from trees near the spot where the C-47 struck the ground and exploded, to prove that the fifth crew member died in the crash."

I knew one of the men who died. He was a crew member who lived in the tent right next to mine. I could have drawn that day's assignment just as easily as he did. The threat hung over us daily since Marshal Josip Broz Tito, Yugoslavia's dictator at the time, was extremely unfriendly to the United States. At least four U.S. aircrafts were shot down from 1945 to 1948. Sadly, their sacrifices generally have been forgotten.

But it wasn't grim all the time. When we had free time, Italy was a wonderful place to be stationed. And I took advantage of the *environment* around me and made sure I had as much *exposure* to another culture as possible.

I had done that everywhere I was stationed. I always have been interested in history, and I took every opportunity to learn about the regions that were my temporary homes. I had a day pass once when I was stationed in Boca Raton in Florida. I wanted to go to Key West, 100 miles from base and another 60 miles into the Keys.

No one wanted to go along, so I went on my own. Gas was rationed, and few cars were on the road. It could have been an exercise in futility. But two middle-aged women picked me up and took me to my destination. I was in uniform, and people wanted to help out servicemen. In addition, people generally just were more trusting then.

In Italy, I set out to see as much of the country as I could. My military driver's license permitted me to drive Jeeps and trucks as small as a quarter-ton and as large as two-tons, the ones where soldiers ride in the back with their equipment.

I went to the Isle of Capri three or four times. I climbed Mount Vesuvius, which had erupted less than a year earlier. Our Italian guide crumpled up a piece of paper and put it into a crevice so we could watch the paper ignite from the heat. I visited Pompeii and Herculaneum, the sites of eruptions centuries earlier.

I knew the toll that war had taken on America's young men. My Aunt Mary's husband Oscar, the man I was riding with just before we learned about Pearl Harbor, lost a nephew in the Bataan Death March in the Philippines. I have pictures of a trip taken to Anzio Beach, and I visited the Sicily-Rome American Cemetery in Nettuno, Italy. There, in the U.S. Military Cemetery, I paid silent tribute at the grave of Private George Ciglarich. He died March 8, 1944, and was awarded the Purple Heart with an oak leaf cluster. He hailed from Virginia, Minnesota, about 100 miles southeast of International Falls. His name sounded familiar to me. In the winter of my senior year in high school, Boy Scouts from around the region had participated in a trip at Crane Lake that *involved* snowshoes and a dog team pulling a sled. George, I think, was one of the Scouts who took part.

Years later, my son Kevin and I took a trip to England and made a pilgrimage to Normandy, site of the 1944 invasion that established Allied forces there. I'm not ashamed to say I cried when we visited the cemetery. There and at Omaha Beach, one of the main landing points for the invasion, I couldn't forget that these young men did not have the opportunities that I had and that it wasn't their choice. But they did their duty.

My military experience was good, but that obviously wasn't always the case for everyone. I think about George Ciglarich and of a fellow I knew from International Falls, Belvidere "Belvie" Arch. He was a playmate from my school days. We would play touch football on the concrete with a gang of boys, and it made no difference to us that Belvie was black. The Arches were the only black family in International Falls. He was one peach of a kid. But when he entered the military, he was segregated from the white population with the other black soldiers. I was told that the experience of being treated as an inferior literally destroyed him. You grow up being somebody, and all of a sudden you're a nobody. Talk about a lesson in human relationships: That was a kid who was one of us, and they destroyed him. I have no idea what happened to Belvie. I would love to know.

But back to Capodichino and my travels. There were two or three trips to Rome. I once had a private audience with Pope Pius XII, with only 10 or 15 others in the room, and I was raised a Protestant! There's a stairwell in St. Peter's Basilica that takes you between the dome's ceiling and roof; I've been up there twice. We had friends who traveled to Rome with us years later. They're Catholic, and I was able to show them around the basilica and take them to the lower level where some of the popes are buried.

I attended opera at La Scalia in Naples. Several of us traveled to Lucerne, Switzerland, where the Swiss welcomed us warmly. A large and modern department store in Zurich, Jelmoli, was so eager to make us feel at home that they printed a pamphlet that had cartoons of American GIs on the cover and a map of the city inside – along with several suggestions of items such as perfume, watches and music boxes we might want to purchase as souvenirs.

Exposure and *involvement.* That's in my blood. As is a zest for adventure. Our squadron commander got his hands on a PT boat. Another fellow and I worked on its radio equipment. Our next trip to Capri, instead of riding on the ferry for four hours, we took the PT boat, and the trip lasted only 30 minutes.

It's about 20 miles around the island. The Blue Grotto is on the north side. The beach is on Capri's southern side, and someone had kayaks to rent there. A buddy and I rented the small boats, and we set out. Our intention was to stop at the Rock of the Sirens to the southeast. Well, when we got to that point, we looked at each other and said, "Let's go," and we set out to circle the island.

Capri's southwest corner consists of sheer cliffs. Unfortunately, that is where my buddy's kayak started to spring a leak, and we had no place to go on shore. I had started to pull his kayak after mine when a motor launch appeared. It was the owner of the kayak-rental place, and, oh, boy, was he mad. He was using every Italian sign there was to express his displeasure! We were not supposed to have done that.

When Rodora and I went back to Italy in 1989, I went down to that beach. The same guy was there, and he remembered that incident. He said then he didn't know of anyone else who had ever paddled around the island.

I ended military service as a three-stripe sergeant. Just before I left Capodichino, it was posted on the headquarters' information board that I was being moved up in rank again: "Sergeant Nyberg will be promoted to staff sergeant." But the promotion never came through. I was going home, and the Air Corps gave it to someone who would stick around.

In December 1946, the International Falls Daily Journal printed a small item, "If you telephone Mrs. Otto Nyberg this week and she sounds a little breathless, please keep in mind that she probably tore to the phone thinking it was son, Roy, calling from New York City. Sergeant Nyberg is enroute (sic) home from Europe and has promised to let his parents know the minute he lands in the States."

I arrived in Italy on February 19, 1946, and I left ten months later. The Army Air Forces gave terminal leave from December 21, 1946, through February 18, 1947. So although my active duty days were over, I remained on the armed forces payroll for almost two months more.

I returned home wearing my military greatcoat. Not many guys were allowed to keep them, but I was heading back to frigid International Falls. They couldn't let me freeze.

I also came home with my military life insurance policy. Every soldier had a $10,000 policy that he paid for automatically. When I left the Army, I kept my insurance policy, something I'll bet 90 percent of the veterans did not. Because if you kept it, you had to pay monthly premiums. I converted mine to a thirty-year pay so when I was 52, I had it paid up. That $10,000 policy today is worth about $80,000. When I tell an insurance agent that I actually still have my GI insurance policy, they tell me, "You're one of a kind."

While I was still in Italy, my mother wrote a letter on September 24, 1946, to the University of Minnesota's Admissions Office. She wanted to know if she could fill out the college application for me so I could start the winter quarter as soon as I returned home. The registrar told her that was permitted.

But about a month before coming home, the University of Minnesota sent another letter. This one informed me that because of my low marks in high school, I would not be accepted into the business administration program. Instead, I would have to enter the university's general college.

I had a decision to make.

To keep myself physically strong, mentally awake, and morally straight

Chapter 8
MY FIRST AND TRUE LOVE

After my stint in the service, I had intended on going to the University of Minnesota. However, the university wasn't as interested in me as I was in it. Officials evidently had checked my high school transcripts, and my past indifference to schoolwork caught up with me. The university did offer to let me enroll in the general college, giving me the chance to prove I could handle more advanced work.

My boyhood buddy, Don Enzman, had been released from the military a year earlier and already was taking classes at the university. He said to me, "Roy, you're already 21 years old. You wouldn't get out of here until you're 25, 26 years of age. Why don't you just go to a two-year business course and not take all this history and stuff we have to take?"

Following his advice, I thereby enrolled at Minneapolis Business College. Since I started school in January 1947 and wasn't discharged until February 1947, technically I still was in the service but didn't have to wear a uniform.

I had reached International Falls on Christmas Eve 1946 glad to be home. But with all of your friends gone, you get bored quickly. Besides, I was anxious to get on with my post-Army Air Forces life. So after a good visit with my parents and becoming reacquainted with my kid brother, Bob, I left for Minneapolis.

Minneapolis Business College offered a two-year course, straight through, with no lengthy summer breaks. But when I started, I told the administration that I was going to follow a different path. I had been away from Rainy Lake, and my family's cabin, for three years, and I wanted to spend the summer there. The administration wasn't happy about that because they didn't expect that I would return. But I knew I would. My goals required college, but my soul needed refreshing in northern Minnesota.

Minneapolis Business College no longer exists. But at that time, it occupied the second and third floors of a building at 10th Street and Nicollet Avenue. A fashionable women's clothing store and furrier, Roy H. Bjorkman's, took up the first floor. The fourth floor was office space.

When you signed up for classes, you were asked if you needed a place to sleep. If you said yes, they would try to find someone in the Minneapolis area who would rent you a bedroom in their home. Housing was tight after World War II, with all the returning servicemen and their families. I told them I would need a place to board., but I wasn't fussy.

When I was asked if I would mind a roommate, I said, no. But I didn't realize that in this instance, "roommate" meant I'd have to share a bed with a total stranger. That was the case at the place I was assigned to, on France Avenue near 50th Street. After one night, I told the landlord I couldn't stay there.

Later that day I mentioned my situation to a classmate, Warren Holcomb. "We've got an extra bedroom," he told me. "Let me talk to Mother." That's how I came to live in the Pleasant Street home of Warren and his parents, Wayne and Ruth Holcomb. Mrs. Holcomb was a sister to W.R. "Win" Stephens, at one time the only Buick dealer in Minnesota. The business exists today as Luther Stephens Buick Pontiac. Mrs. Holcomb was high society, and I was paying her $25 a month for room and board.

The Holcombs treated me like one of the family. We would travel to the nearby town of Shakopee, and they would give me money to play the slot machines. We also would shoot trap on the Stevens farm along the Mississippi River.

Warren was an outgoing individual, and as I spent more time with him, I lost some of the shyness that I had experienced since boyhood. Even in high school I never pushed myself forward. But Warren and I were chosen to make the public announcements to our fellow students at college over the intercom. That *exposure* led to me being more outgoing and gaining enough confident to take on different tasks.

I also benefited from taking an Elmer Wheeler course. He was a 1940s salesman who did research in how the words a salesman uses can affect potential customers. You see that in practice today every time you go to a fast-food restaurant and are asked if you want a large drink instead of being offered a choice of drink sizes. Wheeler's motto was "Don't sell the steak, sell the sizzle." *Involving* myself in that course proved helpful when I began writing the advertising for my own store.

I had returned from my summer at the lake when, shortly after that, the college's coordinator of student facilities was asked to find a student who could help out at the Roy H. Bjorkman's store on our building's lower level. They needed someone to mark merchandise in the receiving room. I took the job and because of that I can joke that I have had my head up more women's slips than anyone else. That is because to put labels on women's half-slips hanging on a rack, I would just throw them over my head and mark the waistband.

As I have said, Bjorkman's was a high-end women's store. You couldn't buy a dress there for less than $100. Its owner, Roy Bjorkman, was a Lincoln, Nebraska, native who had come to Minneapolis in 1923 after meeting designer Philip Mangone, a New York City designer who specialized in coats and suits made of wool. Mangone, a survivor of the Hindenburg disaster, had designed the store at 10th Street and Nicollet Avenue for another retailer who didn't like Minneapolis and returned to Chicago.

When the store was built, Mangone had spent $100,000 on the walnut fixtures alone. Merchandise didn't hang on the racks. Instead, customers relaxed in individual dressing rooms, and the clothing was brought to them. The building, by the way, today houses a restaurant and bar on its main floor. The walnut paneling remains, giving it a warm, rich ambiance. I last was there when my son, Kevin, some of the grandchildren and I went up to see the Minnesota Twins play their final baseball game in the Metrodome in 2009.

Roy Bjorkman was in his upper 50s when he hired me. Despite being enrolled in college, I had plenty of time to take on a part-time job. We went to class and did our assignments, learning how to take care of assets and liabilities, profits and losses, distribution and taxes. With bookkeeping, I didn't have a lot of homework. I think I worked three hours a day after school and on weekends.

After starting in Bjorkman's receiving room, the controller asked me to take care of the purchase book. When invoices came in, I would record how much we owed a company. Eventually the controller who asked me to take that job left for a similar situation with the Ford Motor Company so I moved up to his position.

My *exposure* to the business world played a role in later business practices. Roy Bjorkman understood the value of promotions. He would conduct fashion shows on the interior balcony on the store's south side. One time a Miss America made an appearance there. When I had my own store, promotions immediately became part of what we offered.

I also learned how important sales are to women! When Bjorkman's had a sale, they would mark down those expensive dresses to as low as $25. Women would be waiting outside the door for the store to open. The sales would take place in the balcony, and no one would wait for the elevator. Instead, they would head for the stairs, and heaven help the woman who was slower than the rest!

It was probably the latter part of 1948 when Warren graduated. He was to be married soon, and my time with the Holcombs had to come to an end after 18 months. I was to graduate shortly, too, in January 1949. So I found a rooming house at 3444 Park Avenue run by a woman named Mae Opsal. Bob later stayed in the same rooming house after he graduated from Falls High School and came down to take drafting courses at Dunwoody Institute. Bob and I had started to develop a bond after I returned from the service. We would horse around and wrestle, although it would make my mother nervous. She thought we were going to hurt each other.

I'm glad to say I did develop a true closeness eventually with Bob. But when I was in business college, I was preoccupied with my own interests. One of those interests – it's safe to say my main interest – was a pretty, petite brunette named Rodora Dokken.

The class I started with had 42 graduates, all men. But women attended Minneapolis Business College, too. One day I was sitting with five or six guys, all veterans, in the back of an assembly room when this cute girl comes in and sits within three or four desks of us. To this day she says she had nothing in mind, but I can't believe that! Anyway, I threw a spitball at her and got her attention. Hey, whatever works!

Rodora and her younger brother, Elroy, were raised on a farm near Kenyon, about 55 miles south of the Twin Cities. It's a small town with a population that has remained at 1,600 for decades. Her parents, Elvin and Florence Dokken, were full-blooded Norwegians whose ancestors had come to this country five generations earlier. When I first met her folks, her dad still farmed with horses. He didn't have a tractor, and he drove an old Model A. Their farmhouse did not have indoor plumbing until we were married. There was no way you could say they were a well-to-do farm family. But they were solid, respectable people.

Rodora had graduated from Kenyon High School in May 1948, when she was 17. The very next month she started taking secretarial courses at Minneapolis Business College. Minneapolis was a much, much larger city than she was used to, but she was comforted by the fact she could ride the train home on weekends. Rodora had been interested in working with young children, what today is called early childhood education, and had looked into taking a course in that. But it cost $1,500, and her parents couldn't afford it. Business school was cheaper.

When Rodora graduated from high school she was going with a slightly older boy who had given her a friendship ring when he entered the service. But she never wore it. We talked frequently before and after class. Finally she agreed to go out with me but only on a double date. She says her first reaction to me was that I was a pest, but my persistence paid off! Plus, she says now, she liked the fact that I had goals.

Our first date was in July 1948. We went to the Aquatennial parade, a longtime Minneapolis tradition that would last for hours. Since Rodora didn't want the date to be just the two of us, my brother came down from International Falls and went along with a blind date I arranged for him. We went to the parade, then to Bridgemans on Lyndale Street for ice cream, then to the Theodore Wirth Park for the Aqua Follies, a synchronized swimming demonstration that was popular for more than 20 years until the park equipment needed costly repairs, and it ended.

I have a picture of us on that first date. Rodora has curly bangs and is wearing a dress with a ruffled pinafore and diagonal stripes. On her feet are anklets and saddle shoes. Bob's blind date also is in a dress, and he and I both are attired in neatly pressed white shirts and dress slacks. We looked very sharp.

In the winter, we would go tobogganing. To this day, Rodora can be reluctant to try something new, but once she's *experienced* it, she never hesitates to do it again. It took a long time to coax her to sit behind me on the toboggan, but after the first time she did it she was hooked. Then I had to wheedle her into steering the toboggan for the first time. But once she *experienced* being the lead on a toboggan, I never could do it again!

In the late summer and early fall, we'd go to a park named Excelsior. We'd ride the Ferris wheel and roast sweet corn on outdoor grills. After work we'd go out for malted milks. She says she never put on a pound, but that's when this skinny beanpole first began putting on weight! Rodora and I shared a love for music so we'd go to every musical that came to the Twin Cities. I liked opera so we would go to Northrup Memorial Auditorium on the University of Minnesota campus in Minneapolis. Rodora remembers sitting near women wearing expensive fur coats, and there she was with her cloth coat. But that didn't matter. We always had fun together.

Rodora could have owned a fur coat. With my job at Bjorkman's, I could have made that happen. But she says she's not a fur coat kind of woman. She did buy an expensive Persian paw coat once, which was soft and luxurious, with her own money. In the spring she would take it back to the store in Faribault to be stored until it was cold enough to wear again. But she decided it was too heavy for her taste and sold it to a friend of her mother's.

Rodora was my first girlfriend. If I had ever kissed a girl before Rodora, it was only once or twice. Actually, the first girl I kissed was Barbara Babcock in kindergarten. We were on the street one day after school. I kissed her, and she slapped my face. Years later, at a class reunion, she explained that she had gone to a movie the night before, and when a young man kissed the young lady on screen, she slapped him. The young Barbara thought that was the proper response to a kiss.

But after I met Rodora, I had no interest in ever kissing any other girl, and we soon became inseparable. My wife was a sweetheart then, and she's still a sweetheart. I can't explain what it is about her. She's just an angel.

She had been in school only about three months when the same administrator who found me my job offered her a position with a local business. Rodora began working at Ewald Dairy, taking care of all the government butter records. She hadn't even graduated from anything yet, and she hates bookkeeping. But she goes out there and starts making $250 a month. She's very efficient, very thorough.

I tell people we were engaged in May 1949, but it actually happened months earlier. Of course, this is my version of how it happened. Rodora tells a different story. But I say we were sitting in the car I had purchased from my father, a 1940 Chevrolet. It was 11:45 p.m. on December 31, 1948. Now, 1948 was a leap year, and I told her, "Rodora, you have 15 minutes to ask me to marry you, or you're going to have to wait four years." Because, you know, girls can ask men to marry them in a leap year. So she did.

That spring, we went to a jewelry store half a block down from Bjorkman's, and I bought the ring. It cost me a bundle of money at the time. Rodora wouldn't wear it right away. She wanted her mother to be the first to see the ring. They had a close relationship. Rodora's mother could make her daughter clothing without taking any measurements. The dresses would fit perfectly without any need for alterations. Her mother had harbored concern about our relationship, fearing this farm girl was marrying out of her class. Despite my upbringing in International Falls, Rodora's mother viewed me as a hotshot because I worked for this ritzy clothing store.

When we drove to see her folks, just before reaching the farm I pulled over near an orchard of blooming apple trees and slipped the ring on her finger.

Rodora's mother made her wedding dress, and we were married in Gol Lutheran Church at Kenyon on September 16, 1950. Rodora was 19, I was 24. My brother, Bob, was my best man, and a cousin and my old friend Skeezix Enzman were the groomsmen. Rodora's maid of honor was a girl she had met at college. They didn't stay in touch long, and Rodora now regrets she didn't ask someone whose friendship would have continued over the years.

We wanted to keep our honeymoon destination secret, but Bob found a card in his dresser that gave the location. When he took us to nearby Faribault, where I had my car hidden, he told us to have a nice time in the Black Hills of South Dakota. Bob says our jaws dropped when we learned our secret had gotten out. When he was married, I found out where he and Char were going to stay in Duluth and mailed a card to greet them on their arrival. But I didn't know they had changed their reservations to a hotel in Superior, so that joke was on me.

Rodora had lived in a dorm on Grant Avenue while attending college, one that had an 11:00 p.m. curfew on weekends, and the first time I ever got inside that door was after we were married and I went upstairs to get her personal belongings. The women who oversaw her dorm never permitted men inside.

After going on our honeymoon to the Black Hills, we came back to our first residence, an apartment on Plymouth Avenue. But it wouldn't be our home for long.

A Scout is ... trustworthy and loyal

Chapter 9

FROM A HONEYMOON TO HIBBING

Rodora and I were going to begin married life financially secure. She was earning $250 a month at her job at Ewald's Dairy, and Roy H. Bjorkman's was paying me a monthly wage of $500 as its controller.

But I wasn't completely happy working for the clothing store. My boss, Roy Bjorkman, was a showman and a spendthrift. He was playing the high-society angle. But our financial practices weren't always by the book. I remember once we had an order for a $6,000 fur coat, and the company in New York City refused to ship it because we were paying our bills 120 days late. That's four months out! He had me send two fur capes to the top men at a national credit reporting company so we could get our credit rating improved.

But at the same time, the old man – he was probably just in his early 50s, but that's how I thought of him – had to make splashy gestures. An airline offered a brand-new luxury flight from Minneapolis to New York City, and he had to be on that, even though we were behind in paying our creditors. Those were not the values I grew up with and certainly not the business ethics I learned at Rudy Erickson's hardware store.

I started applying for other positions. After I graduated from Minneapolis Business College, I applied for a job in management with Gamble-Skogmo, a conglomerate of general merchandise stores. But when I told them I had only a two-year degree, they turned me down. The only applicants they would take seriously had bachelor's degrees. You've got to remember, they had all these men coming back after the war, and I suppose a lot of them were four-year graduates, looking for work at the same time I was. Employers could be choosy – rightly or wrongly!

Then I applied at Warner Hardware, which had about 25 stores in Minneapolis. I wanted to go there as a manager, not as a receiving clerk or a salesman because I had a college background. But again, they were hiring only people with a bachelor's degree.

What is ironic is that Gamble-Skogmo is no longer in existence; I outshone them in many respects when I entered business on my own. But what's really ironic is that after I trained Jody, my oldest daughter, she moved to Minneapolis and was hired by Warner Hardware. Jody worked her way up to become Warner Hardware's first female manager, even though she had only one year of college. But she had good experience – I'd trained her in my hardware store! Not having a four-year degree never held Jody back.

In a letter dated March 22, 1950, I responded to a newspaper ad seeking a manager and listed my responsibilities at Bjorkman's: in charge of personnel; purchasing of all supplies for the store, which had a yearly volume of more than $1 million and employed 100 people; responsible for records and accounting procedures. I also supervised ten people.

Later that year, I also wrote to my old boss, Rudy Erickson in International Falls. In a visit to International Falls in March 1950, Rudy had mentioned he was making tentative plans to open another hardware store in Northwestern Minnesota, and I asked about any possible positions in that store.

"I'm getting married in September and my fiancee and myself both have the desire to live in a small town not being entirely happy here in a large city," I wrote. "So Mr. Erickson if there is anything open or if you know of any position would you please inform me. I would be grateful to you." I don't remember if I ever had a reply to that letter.

Before our marriage, Rodora and I rented a place on Plymouth Avenue in North Minneapolis. It was a two-story house converted into apartments. We had a living room and a little nook to cook in, and we shared the bathroom with the other renters on our floor. Our bed was in the living room. It was a pull-out couch my folks gave us as a wedding gift.

Now, when I say we rented a place, that doesn't mean we moved in together. Not a chance! That was a no-no when we were young. I treated Rodora with respect. I'm not saying we didn't have our hugs and kisses and steam up the car! But otherwise, no way! You did not – if you had a good woman like I had – screw it up. You did not want her to toss you aside.

I never had been to South Dakota, but that was our choice of a honeymoon destination. It was a popular destination for a lot of young couples. Our first night we stayed at the Burton Hotel in Mankato. After going to church the next morning, we traveled to Mitchell, South Dakota, for the second night and reached the Black Hills on Monday. We stayed at what is now the Sylvan Lake Lodge for three days, then headed back, spending a night in Aberdeen. We were going to International Falls for a few days so Mother could have an open house and show off my bride to her friends.

On our way back to Minneapolis, we stopped in Hibbing. I had never seen the store that I was supposed to help open in the summer of 1944, and I was curious. I wanted to show the store to Rodora, too. I can't tell you if I had it in my mind to ask Harvey Remer if I could come back there and work when I proposed the trip to Hibbing. But that's what I did when we met again.

Harvey Remer had a 49 percent ownership in the store and Rudy Erickson 51 percent. The store in Hibbing offered furniture in conjunction with the hardware part, and they also sold appliances. Appliances were a big part of the business. Right after the war, any appliance you could get, you could sell.

The Hibbing store had three department managers, and thanks to my persistence and my connection with Rudy Erickson and Harvey Remer – the man I had trained when I was in high school – over the years, I was offered one of those jobs. Basically I would be in charge of sporting goods and of hardware and tools, and I would supervise the paint and housewares departments. Archie Hemming ran the plumbing and electrical departments and Harold Nordeen, a Swede with a strong accent, had the furniture.

The offer Harvey made to me was this: I would have a salary of $250 a month, and we three supervisors would split 50 percent of the profits over what Rudy and Harvey considered was a fair return on their investment. I have no idea what they considered a fair return; we had to rely on their integrity. And I knew I could. Actually, my income became sufficient enough that we paid for a new ranch-style home in six years' time.

Keep in mind, Rodora and I would have earned a combined $750 a month at our jobs in Minneapolis. But this was my chance to return to the hardware business, which I truly missed and felt comfortable in. We didn't hesitate. I took the job. When we came back to Minneapolis after our honeymoon, we gave notice at our jobs. We lived in our first apartment less than two months before we moved to Hibbing for our initial adventure as a married couple.

A Scout is...courteous and kind

Chapter 10

FIREARMS AND A DETOUR

Much of my ability to think positively and to look for opportunities came, I think, from being *exposed* to the business acumen of Rudy Erickson and Harvey Remer. But I have always benefited from learning from the people around me. They provided an *environment* that encouraged me as a boy and as a young man. I've never forgotten the words of a elderly man in Hibbing who told me, speaking with a Ukrainian accent, "Never buy a thing unless you go first class; it only costs a tenth of a percent more."

Ida Gilsoul was a good first teacher at the hardware store in International Falls, and in Minneapolis I learned a lot from Bernice Bishop, the credit manager at Roy H. Bjorkman's. She is in her 90s now, still living in Minneapolis, and we have remained in contact all these years.

Perhaps that is why the one co-worker with whom I had a run-in remains so vivid. Archie Hemming already was employed with the Ace Hardware store in Hibbing when I started in 1950. I don't think I was flaunting my previous association with Rudy and Harvey, but maybe that's how Archie saw it. He was quite proficient in his responsibilities, the plumbing and electrical departments, but maybe my earlier relationship with the owners intimidated him or caused him uneasiness.

In any case, one day after I'd been there some months, his irritation spilled over in the office, and we almost got into a fist fight. When I say that, I mean we didn't actually touch each other, but he was angry enough to swing at me. I have always been a peaceable sort of individual, and I'm just not one to fight. But in the end, he got whatever unhappiness he felt off his chest, and we got along after that. In fact, we became good friends.

In addition to the departments I managed, I also oversaw the paint and housewares departments. I assisted the women assigned to those two areas and did all the ordering and merchandising for my own areas, sporting goods and hardware and tools.

Back in the 1950s, the Ace in Hibbing reportedly was the first self-service hardware store in the state. In that era, and especially in Minneapolis, that was the beginning of the age of discount stores – not just in hardware but all retailers. Rudy and Harvey recognized that this was the trend. They knew they had to keep up with the times, or the store would lose its customer base. Our store in Hibbing was 50 feet wide and half a block deep. For that era, it was one of the premier hardware stores. Rudy believed a store owner needed to make changes and show improvements annually. That was particularly important coming out of the Depression and the war years when stores looked the same for 20 years. He recommended freshening up a store regularly to make it more appealing. That's why customers will come into a store and find items have moved once again.

I was working for two men with vision, and I never forgot that.

In the meantime, Rodora and I were settling into life in Hibbing, which had a population of about 16,000 residents in 1950. Hibbing had been founded in 1893 by a German miner who discovered iron ore. The town was moved two miles south, beginning in 1919, after iron ore was discovered under the original location.

Hibbing has several claims to fame. It is called the Grand Canyon of the North, because it is the site of the world's largest open pit iron ore mine. The Greyhound Bus Line was founded in Hibbing. And it also is the boyhood home of musician Bob Dylan. His dad, Abe Zimmerman, owned a family business in Hibbing, an electrical and appliance store on 5th Avenue, just off Howard Street. Bob would come in the store to pick up items for his family's store, and I would wait on him. He was just another customer, just this kid. I don't even remember him having any musical talent. But a friend of Rodora's told us at the time that the high school principal, who was her father, pulled the curtain on Bob during a performance. The high school had a Steinway piano, and Bob was playing the Jerry Lee Lewis rock 'n' roll song, "Great Balls of Fire," with all the key-pounding zest for which Lewis was known. School administrators were fearful Bob would damage their Steinway!

As it had been in Minneapolis, housing continued to be hard to find when we moved to Hibbing. We ended up in a made-over neighborhood grocery store. The front part of it was ours. We put our wedding gift of a hideaway couch in the living room, and it had a kitchen and a storage room that would have been the bedroom if we'd had a real bed.

After only a few months we moved to a second apartment, again in a building that had not been designed for multiple tenants. We divided one room into a bedroom and living room. You could see our bed from the living room. A drape could have been hung from wall to wall to separate the two, but we never got it done. I used some of the money I had saved in high school to buy a lot in Hibbing, but we never built a house on it. Instead we moved into a ranch-style house, only a year old, and took on a $9,000 mortgage in 1954.

By that time our family had grown. Jody LaRae was born November 27, 1951, while we lived in our second apartment in Hibbing, followed by Nancy Gail on June 10, 1954. Kevin Roy was born after we moved into the house at 3911 4th Avenue E. on December 13, 1956. We didn't complete our family for ten more years until Marin Kay was born July 12, 1966, in Sioux Falls.

When we moved to Hibbing, Rodora took a job at an office supply company. But she did not like being a bookkeeper and quit after about a month. It is one of the few times I can ever remember her quitting anything. That's just not her personality. But it was okay. We soon found out our first child was on its way.

But even without her income, she made things work. Our food budget was no more than $35 a month, and she could stretch it to a marvel.

In Hibbing, with Rodora's support at home, I began my *involvement* in community activities. And it was because of Rodora that I became a member of Our Savior's Lutheran Church in Hibbing. Rodora's faith, nurtured in a small church near Kenyon, led me to look more closely at my own beliefs, or lack thereof.

I did not grow up in a particularly religious home. The first church I remember attending was a Swedish Lutheran church in International Falls. The pastor was a missionary from Canada, and he would preach against cards, movies and shows, and dancing. If you participated in any of those things, he would thunder from the pulpit, you were leaving the good Lord outside.

My dad balked at that. He said that wasn't the way he'd been taught religion in Sweden, and besides, he loved two of the three forbidden activities: cards and dancing. (A side note: In March 2010, Rodora and I were attending Lord of Life Lutheran Church in Surprise, Arizona. After services, I struck up a conversation with a parishioner. She told me her husband was born in International Falls. When he joined the conversation, he mentioned he was the son of a pastor. Turns out, his father was Charles Matson, the preacher at the Swedish Lutheran church and also a pastor for a church over the border in Fort Francis. When I shared my story with him, he said, "Yes, my dad disliked movies and dancing." What a small world it can be!)

Mother and Dad were married in the Methodist church in International Falls, although back in Tennessee her family were Baptists, so I don't know why they didn't continue with that denomination. But we didn't join the Methodists either. We ended up going to Bethlehem Congregational Church. I took part in a Bible camp one summer and participated in Sunday school. But I never felt like I had received a strong religious training. There was no confirmation class or program where we could learn about Jesus, just the coloring of Bible pictures. That may be one reason why my *experience* with Boy Scouts was so important. Scouting laws and rules gave me something to hang on to and live by; a moral compass.

Even to this day, I feel I am lacking in a proper religious background. But after meeting Rodora and becoming involved in her Lutheran church, I found a certain peace I had been missing. To this day, I have to go to church on Sunday or I don't feel prepared adequately for the coming week.

So I became active at Our Savior's Lutheran Church in Hibbing to the extent that I served as a deacon. Our Savior's was a fifty-year-old church in the middle of a growth spurt. In 1953 it moved into its new building; a few years later I became building chairman for the new Sunday school wing.

The pastor there was the Rev. J.T. "Jake" Stolee. We used to call him Rabbi Stolee. He was a great guy. He was a man who understood men, and you liked him for reasons that went beyond his spiritual leadership. We became such good personal friends that he would come down to the store, and we'd go out for coffee. He later made me an offer I've never forgotten.

Another major *involvement* was with the state firearms safety program.

I never hunted much as a boy, maybe two or three times. You didn't do it for recreation. It was the Depression, and you didn't waste money on bullets. I do recall going out several times as a boy with a friend named Harry Poster. We were out in Dad's '33 Chevy, probably hunting grouse, with .22 rifles. Harry saw a couple ducks on Black Bay and hollered at me to stop. But in his excitement, he caught the trigger mechanism on the interior door handle, and the gun fired! He was lucky since the shell whizzed between his arm and his body.

On that same trip, Harry told me to stop at a gravel pit on our way back to town. He said he just wanted to see if any deer were around. He was right: Several deer were there. He started taking shots at them and killed one. This was out of season, and illegal. I was as scared as you could be. But he put the carcass in my car, and with meat rationing in effect, my folks welcomed the deer meat for the supper table.

I have always said, if your father doesn't hunt, chances are that as an adult you won't become a hunter either. But I proved the exception to my own rule. I started hunting as an adult because I was put in charge of Ace's sporting goods department, and I needed to know the merchandise. Good friends from Hibbing, Boyd Angen and Eldon

Sougstad, and I did a lot of hunting together, deer primarily, sometimes grouse. I never have cared for duck hunting.

In 1955, Minnesota started a firearms safety program for youngsters. How I got *involved* in it I don't recall, but I became the first volunteer firearms safety director for northern St. Louis County.

Keep in mind, St. Louis County is vast, the largest county east of the Mississippi River. Duluth, its county seat, was 76 miles away so an auxiliary courthouse is located in Hibbing. For the firearms safety program, we split the county just south of Hibbing, and I was in charge of everything to the north. That includes about 20 towns such as Chisholm, Buhl, Virginia, Tower Soudan, Eveleth and Ely. We went as far north as Silver Bay on Lake Superior.

To make the program successful, I had to have instructors in all of these towns. As director, I would make sure they had the necessary equipment such as film projectors and ammunition. We set up meetings to train our instructors, and I worked closely with Louis Peloquin, the state game warden in our area.

After a slow start, in eight months' time St. Louis County had trained more youngsters in the proper use of firearms than any of Minnesota's other 79 counties. It took a lot of my time, so you can imagine how proud I was when we were named the most outstanding firearms safety program in Minnesota in both 1956 and 1957.

In the meantime, my work at the store also took up many hours. Rudy Erickson came to Hibbing once a month. He had started in business with very little and became quite successful, probably making more of his money from the furniture stores he owned than the hardware stores. In the end, he ended up owning eight or ten Kordel furniture stores in northern Minnesota.

He and Harvey Remer had talked about taking in we three department managers as partners, but the months passed and nothing came of it. I could see that the hardware stores weren't receiving as much attention as the furniture stores, and I was becoming restless.

It was time to take action. It was time to have my own store.

A Scout is...clean and reverent

Chapter 11

FOURTEEN YEARS FROM DREAM TO REALITY

Hibbing was an interesting town in which to live. There were large dump sites where the overburden from the ore pit had been deposited. While we were there, the pit owners were starting to dig into the dumps because a new taconite process could recover ore that earlier had not been pure enough to use. Our firearms safety program set up a target range on the eastern end of Hibbing's main street, and amazingly enough, live ammunition was fired there.

Like International Falls, Hibbing had a strong immigrant population, largely Finns, Norwegians and Swedes with Italians and others thrown in for seasoning. Many of them lived in houses that rimmed the mine, so when these men went to work all they had to do was step out of their house and walk right down into the pits. In the early years, they shoveled ore by hand; there were no steam engines. Things progressively got better.

Hibbing was a melting pot of various nationalities, and its cuisine reflected that. Our church, Our Savior's Lutheran, would hold lutefisk suppers and also serve pasties, a meat pie sealed in a crust that had originated in Cornwall in the United Kingdom.

I might have been content there if Rudy Erickson and Harvey Remer had given any indication of letting me, and the other two department managers, become partners. Rudy and Harvey had talked of opening a new hardware store in another community. But nothing was coming of it, nor did it look like anything was going to happen soon.

After about six years in Hibbing, I began to look for a store of my own. Rodora and I took a vacation to North Dakota where a man named Charlie Crawford owned seven or eight stores. He was interested in me becoming one of his manager-partners. But I didn't feel the same interest, and that decision turned out to be the right one. Some time later Charlie Crawford was killed in the crash of the plane he was piloting, and soon his whole empire was gone.

That same trip we also went to Torrington, Wyoming, where an older couple was looking to sell their hardware store. I don't know why I didn't get more excited about that opportunity. Maybe I just was afraid of the barren West. I also looked at a store in Cloquet, Minnesota, but again, something held me back.

In the fall of 1957, I attended the annual meeting of the state firearms safety program in Minneapolis. The next morning, I planned on leaving Minneapolis and heading back to Hibbing, with a stop at the St. Louis County Courthouse in Duluth. Usually, my route would have been on Highway 53, which goes straight to Duluth. But there was a detour that took me off the main road and past an industrial park that housed Frost Paint Company, the supplier of Ace Hardware's private-label paint. A right turn would put me on the Frost Paint grounds.

I knew the two principles at Frost Paint Company, Doug Manuel and Don Ottenweller, quite well. Doug was president, Don the national sales manager. I was so close to Don that I had asked him earlier if he would watch for any hardware stores that were for sale.

I had never been to the paint factory before, and I was curious to see it. But I also knew if I stopped, they would want me to go out to coffee or to lunch, and I didn't think I should spare the time.

But, almost on impulse, I pulled in. That decision to make a right turn instead of going left made a world of difference in the rest of my life.

Because sure enough, they said, "Let's go to Jack's," a nearby restaurant. And while we were talking, Don snapped his fingers and said, "Roy, there's a store in Sioux Falls, South Dakota, that you should look at."

I can remember that so vividly. And even though at one point when I was in the Army Air Forces I'd almost been sent to Sioux Falls, I'd forgotten that and said, "South Dakota? Sioux Falls? Where the hell is that!"

We talked a little longer, then I headed up to Duluth.

Right after that conversation, I was scheduled to take a vacation. I'd planned a trip into the Boundary Waters, taking a motorboat up there with two friends, Boyd Angen and Eldon Sougstad. In those days the wilderness area regulations weren't as strict so we could fish in something other than a canoe.

But before I left, I took the time to write to Ed Howlin, the owner of the Ace Hardware store on Minnesota Avenue in Sioux Falls. I said that I had heard his store was for sale and that I was interested in learning more about it.

When I returned, I had a letter waiting from Ed, asking me to come to Sioux Falls.

My boss, Harvey Remer, had flown to Cuba on vacation. Since I was in charge of the Hibbing store in his absence. I couldn't be gone long. So after I closed the store on a Saturday night, Rodora and I drove to Sioux Falls, accompanied by a friend, Roger Ronning, who offered to help me navigate the 400 miles. It was all two-lane roads at that time, so it took us about seven hours.

Ed had owned the store only since the previous February. He had had a heart attack in April, and the doctor had told him the stress was too much. To save his life, he needed to get rid of the store.

We met Ed and Alice at their home at 10:00 a.m. Sunday, ate dinner at the Ming Wah restaurant in downtown Sioux Falls, and by 2:00 p.m., we were done talking. I told Ed that I wanted to buy the store. I could barely contain my eagerness and impatience. The store's price was right, and the terms Ed was offering were fair. In only a few hours I had made a decision that would change my life. It was impulsive, and that is out of character for me. But it felt right. And Rodora and I always have shared the same attitude: Life is an adventure!

Ed, however, wasn't ready to move quite so quickly. He flat-out told me to hold on a bit. "I've got to find out more about who you are," he said.

Rodora, Roger Ronning and I turned around and headed back to Hibbing because I had to be there to open the hardware store on Monday morning.

But after that things progressed swiftly. I needed to find enough money for the down payment. I had $13,000 of my own and would have more after we sold our house in Hibbing. I think I paid Ed about $37,000 for the inventory. My father lent me $13,000, and I put that in the bank and used it when I needed ready access to cash. I paid him six percent interest, which is more than he would have gotten from a bank, and every month I sent him a payment.

I said earlier that our church pastor was a good guy. I now can break a promise I made to Pastor Jake Stolee more than 50 years ago. During the period that I was looking for a store of my own, I had confided in him about my search. He also was a good friend of my boss Harvey. But he never told Harvey a thing about my plans. And he made me a generous offer. "Roy, if you aren't able to swing this deal," he said, "I'll be a silent partner with you." He had such faith in me that he was offering to lend me money. I never needed his help, but I've never forgotten his offer. I promised that even if I didn't need his help, I would never divulge his offer until after his death. And I didn't.

I purchased the store's inventory from Ed Howlin on a contract for deed. We shared an attorney, Nils Boe, who was a state legislator at the time and later served as South Dakota's governor. Boe told me my Hibbing attorney wouldn't do, that I had to have an attorney in South Dakota. When I asked, "Can't you represent us both?," he thought for a minute and agreed. He was equally fair to us, pointing out what in the contract benefited Ed and what benefited me.

By the way, buying a store's inventory on contract for deed is almost unheard of. If I wanted to, I could have sold the inventory off and absconded with the proceeds. Years later, I asked Ed why he sold me the inventory that way.

He said, "Well, two reasons, Roy. First of all, you had been Ace-ified." That meant I knew how the Ace program worked, every bit of it. My education in all things Ace had started when I was 16 and living in International Falls. Again, it's that *involvement, environment* and *exposure.*

The second reason? Ed said he knew he could trust me because I was an Eagle Scout. My *involvement* in Scouting certainly paid off!

On December 26, 1957, I left Hibbing to move to Sioux Falls. Rodora intended to stay in Hibbing until we sold our house on 4th Avenue.

Pastor Stolee of Our Savior's Lutheran in Hibbing did one more favor for me. He suggested that when we moved to Sioux Falls, we attend the Our Savior's Lutheran Church there. Its senior pastor, the Rev. Howard Blegen, was a seminary classmate of his. I attended my first service there on New Year's Eve of 1957, and it was our church home for 42 years.

When I first reached Sioux Falls, I rented a room at the YMCA, which at that time had space – essentially cubbyholes – on its third and fourth floors. The Y charged, if I'm not mistaken, a dollar a night, and we renters shared a community shower. After a week there, I found a house to rent near 27th Street and Duluth Avenue. In January 1958 I moved in and began painting the interior and preparing it for Rodora and the children. They were going to wait and move when the Hibbing house sold. But after a few weeks, I said, "I don't care. I'm coming to get you anyway." And then the house sold! They arrived in mid-February 1958. Jody was in kindergarten, Nancy and Kevin too young for school.

Rodora tells this story as an example of how impressed she was with Sioux Falls. Jody started school Friday, February 14, 1958, at Mark Twain Elementary – Valentine's Day. The teacher told her pupils on Thursday that a new classmate was joining them the next day. Jody came home from school Friday with valentines from everyone in her room.

When I took over the store, which was in a strip mall on Minnesota Avenue named Southway Shopping Center, one of the things I insisted on was making sure the street numbers were large and easy to see. A big 2111 was painted on the transom. It always bugs me when businesses don't make their address easy to find, and I didn't want people having to search for 2111 S. Minnesota Avenue.

It was my store, and I was going to make sure people knew how to find it.

A Scout is...brave and trustworthy

Chapter 12

THAT'S THE WAY WE PLANNED IT

When I bought the store on Minnesota Avenue, it was simply named Ace Hardware. I changed it to Nyberg's Ace Hardware in 1969, as a way of protecting myself. As my store started to grow and as Ace started to grow, I just felt if there was ever a day I wanted to tell Ace to go fly a kite, Nyberg's would be a name that people trusted, and all I would have to do is change the supplier's name.

Don't get me wrong, though. Ace is a good hardware chain. I've always been proud to be associated with it.

During World War II, between hardware retailers and hardware wholesalers in Sioux Falls, the phone book contained 21 listings. When I came to town in 1958, there were 11 what I considered full-fledged hardware retailers. Today, there are five traditional hardware stores, and we have four of them: Robson Hardware and the Nyberg's Ace stores on Minnesota, Sertoma and Sycamore Avenues and 12th Street.

I didn't know how many competitors I would have when I came to Sioux Falls, however. I didn't take any surveys the way a person normally would or check out the neighborhood. I guess it was just luck that I got the store that I did. Somebody was smiling down on me.

But I never did anything to put any of my competitors out of business. That's not my style. We just did our thing.

And my "thing" was to draw in everyone.

I had purchased the store from Ed Howlin, who bought it from a man named Andy Westra. Westra had operated a Marshall Wells hardware store for some time, but he told me years later that he had become fearful for his store's future when a Lewis Drug Store had opened nearby, on 35th Street.

There were two other hardware stores only blocks away, too. But I didn't know that when I bought the store from Ed. I didn't know about Lewis Drug, which was going to offer a bit of everything, riding a new wave in retailing at the time. I just wanted my own hardware store, and badly.

Southway Shopping Center, the strip mall where I was located, had various retailers, with Sam's Super Valu grocery anchoring the 30th Street corner. In 1958, the mall included a camera store, a florist, a beauty shop, a laundromat and a carpet store. An A&W root beer stand occupied the corner of 29th Street and Minnesota Avenue.

We weren't a big store at 4,000 square feet, probably the size of the Ace Hardware in International Falls, not as big as the store in Hibbing. Soon I built on a shanty on the north side and installed a door so customers would have easy access to our lawn and garden department.

Any store needs good employees, and I've mostly been fortunate in my workers. Part of being a good boss is having the ability to size up a job applicant's character. One instance when it looked like I'd been wrong happened when I came to work one morning, and the safe had been taken from the back room.

We found it in the basement. Someone had taken tools from my own store to open my own safe! The police quickly determined that it had been an inside job, and the thief turned out to be one of my employees, a teenage boy. He also had been stealing wallets from cars parked in the mall parking lot.

But when it came time to prosecute, I didn't. In fact, I kept him on as an employee. All I can say now is, I thought he deserved a second chance. He made the most of it, too. I see him frequently. He never has acknowledged his past misdeeds. But he is married, nearing retirement age, and he raised a couple good kids. I made the right decision.

Another time I hired a young man named Jim Tollefson who had served time in prison. He had a younger girlfriend whose father didn't like him. When he took the girlfriend across the state line, the father had him prosecuted for violating the Mann Act, designed to prevent white slavery.

Jim became a good employee. He was very outgoing, very polite. I never had any problems with him. When he did leave my employ, it was to take a job at True Value headquarters in Illinois. His experience at my hardware store had made him a desirable employee to others.

I may not have tried to put anyone out of business, but that doesn't mean I didn't take part in a lively competition for customers. When I came to Sioux Falls, Lewis Drug Store was selling an aluminum grain scoop for $6.99. There wasn't a farmer in the state who didn't know about Lewis' $6.99 grain scoops.

Not only that, but O.A. Ames & Company, now known as Ames True Temper and the oldest manufacturer of hand tools and garden tools in the United States, was well aware of Lewis. And they knew those grain shovels weren't theirs. So I'm at an Ace buying show in Chicago, and Ames' national sales manager sees by my name tag that I'm from Sioux Falls, South Dakota.

He grabs me by my jacket lapels and orders, "Come here!" He says, "I want you to take this aluminum shovel back to Sioux Falls, and I want you to sell it for $5.99!" I say, "Okay, I'll take a dozen." That's me, a big spender!

I think I paid $4.99 for the grain scoops, so I stood to make a dollar profit. The Lewis manager came up to me at a Kiwanis meeting after I had advertised our bargain and says, "What are you doing with our grain scoop?" I answer back, "What are YOU doing selling my grain scoop?" And I added, "I'll tell you what, you lower your price, and I'm going to guarantee you, I'll go down a dollar lower." That was the end of it. I sold my initial dozen and I don't know how many more because we just took over the grain scoop market.

We weren't part of downtown, but the retail area in Sioux Falls was expanding outside of Phillips and Main avenues. Courtney E. Anderson, whose grandfather founded Southway Shopping Center, says it is one of the oldest strip malls in Sioux Falls if not the oldest. By the way, its original name was Southdale Mall, but a group of investors from Minneapolis who were starting a major retail mall with a Dayton's department store inside bought the rights to that name from Courtney's grandfather. Park Ridge Shopping Center, the oldest enclosed strip mall, had been built at Western Avenue and 26th Street in 1955, but the retail mall where I was located, Southway Shopping Center, had opened almost five years earlier, in about 1950.

I set out to make sure people knew we were there. I started the first Crazy Daze sale in Sioux Falls in the late 1960s, and we made a big deal of it. Other Southway stores followed suit, and for a few years we even had a parade downtown. I've got a picture of myself in a red wagon, wearing a diaper and sucking on a pacifier. Another time I put on a red wig and a ballerina outfit. All my staff dressed up, and we would have costume contests for the youngsters. Crazy Daze wasn't a new idea; no idea is new. But no one had done it in Sioux Falls before I proposed it.

The importance of bringing the store to newcomers' attention was recognized. We sent welcome cards to new residents offering a gift plus a free key to their front door. Free front-door keys also were offered to city residents who moved to a new location.

We were innovators in promotions. One year we had a snowstorm, back when Minnesota Avenue still was only two lanes. Snow was piled high up on the boulevard. I threw artificial grass on top of the seven-foot-high snow pile, then put a lawnmower on top of that. The local newspaper took a picture of it, and The Associated Press picked it up so it ran elsewhere.

Another year, tying in with Sioux Falls' annual city beautification campaign called "Spruce Up," I ran one letter from that phrase in a newspaper ad on eight consecutive days, along with a bingo-type card. The first 50 people who brought in the completed card received a fifty-foot garden hose. We ran out of those hoses within two hours of opening on the final day.

I had people assist me with these promotions, both to put them on and to help me understand their value. I remember making a speech once to about 2,000 people where I said, when you put on a promotion, it's like putting on a stage play. When you raise the curtain, it's showtime, and you don't want to leave anything undone.

An ad salesman in Hibbing first helped me see the value of advertising. In Sioux Falls, two other men continued to help me learn about advertising's importance. The late Verl Thomson owned KISD radio station out on 12th Street. He had a deep voice and a winning way, and he was a strong supporter of advertising on radio. Working with him was a salesman named LeRoy Okerlund. When he came to sell me radio advertising, he had an entire promotional format for me to consider. It wasn't just radio advertising, it was a follow-through for everything we needed to do.

We advertised on local radio stations, relying on humor to get our message across. Nyberg's Ace Hardware also was one of the smaller stores to start advertising on television. I would go downtown at noon to KELO, where Gena Hartig hosted a live noontime show. There was no retaping if a mistake was made. I'd have a minute to talk about whatever I wanted. One day – I'll never forget this – I brought down some Corningware dishes. The company had just come out with dishware that they boasted was unbreakable and could go right in the oven.

Before the program I was flipping these dishes all over their concrete floor. Right in the middle of a live spot, I threw one of them on the floor, and CRASH! It shattered into a thousand pieces. When it was quiet again, I said quickly, "And if that happens, it's guaranteed!" I didn't even have to take a breath.

Humor was important in TV ads, too. I got sick and tired of Father's Day coming around, and kids being told that one of the better items to buy their dad was a TIE! I can remember going down to Cliff Avenue, at the curve of the river, and putting one of my ties on a fishing rod and casting it into the water for a TV commercial.

We billed everyone on the staff as "lawn doctors," and our ads would show white-coated "physicians" fixing lawn mowers, slow-to-grow lawns and other problems. We would advertise "free house calls," telling homeowners to call us whenever they had a problem and we would diagnose it. Signs on the Ace truck said, "Prescription delivery from the lawn doctors."

In 1983 I attended a family reunion, and a cousin suggested we sell Colorado peaches. That first year we only sold 500 lugs. Now we sell 5,000 lugs! We also had family hunters' stags for years, and we brought the world's fastest quick-draw artists in for demonstrations. The idea of free acts later was picked up by the local fair board.

See why our slogan was "Don't chase, Ace is the place"?

I learned something during one promotion: Keep it at your store. Once, after we had moved to 41st Street and Minnesota Avenue, we offered a lawn-care clinic at Dan Dugan's tank farm on West 41st Street where it was open grass. But it was a mile away from the store, and no one came to it. That's when I found out if you're going to have a promotion, have customers come to your premises. Even when you have a dud, you can learn from it.

We never hesitated to try something different. We brought Weber kettles, the barbecue grills, to Sioux Falls. Weber kettles were in their infancy when I came to town, and nobody had them here. Other stores offer them now, but we still sell Weber kettles by the truckload.

When you walked into my store in the strip mall on Minnesota Avenue, you saw housewares to the left. On the right wall was sporting goods, and not even 40 feet down the center was general merchandise, sold seasonally. Then we had to have lawn and garden, plumbing, tools and galvanized ware. The store was packed. We had a lot to offer.

We still do. One Sunday before Christmas 2009, I picked up the Ace circular from our daily paper, the Argus Leader, just the way any customer would do. I'm serious: It took me all of 20 to 25 minutes to get to the back page. There were so many items customers might be interested in that I even got interested myself.

Keep in mind, Ace Hardware primarily has paint, tools, plumbing, electrical, hardware, lawn and garden, that's it. So when you get an Ace corporate circular, that's what you're going to see. But I wanted to make sure my store had something for everyone. I put in items that would draw in men, women and children, whole families.

At Christmastime, we became known for our toy selection. Ace offered its dealers toys, but it had just the major toy manufacturers, nothing you couldn't get anywhere else. One year I was at a seminar in Las Vegas and became acquainted with a wholesaler called Worldwide Distributors, and it became a second source of a supply for merchandise. That's another reason why we do as well as we do: We're just not a man's store.

My store in the Southway Shopping Center had something for everybody. But, as I said, it was crowded. It was time to expand.

A Scout is...helpful and courteous

Chapter 13
TRIUMPH AND TRAGEDY, 1969-1972

Sioux Falls was growing rapidly in the 1960s, and business was moving away from the downtown area where Phillips Avenue had two to three blocks of stores. Some of that expansion came to Minnesota Avenue, where my store was located.

One day a downtown menswear salesman named Norman Severson came to talk with me. He was employed with a clothing store on Phillips Avenue, but he wanted to go out on his own.

Norm said to me, "What do you think if I were to come out here and put a clothing store in?" I responded, "Well, there's no men's clothing store outside of downtown. I don't think it would be such a bad idea."

In the fall of 1967, he opened a store in the same strip mall where I was located, taking over the storefront where Around-the-Clock Laundromat had been located. He later moved to a nearby building, off 35th Street, because the first store was next door to Southway Cafe, and odors from the cooked food wafted through the walls and clung to his merchandise.

Southway Shopping Center had shown a lot of stability since I moved in. Dakota Business Machines still was there, along with Anderson Flowers, Bill Pay's Camera Shop and Vernita's Salon of Beauty. The A&W stood to the north, although in a sign of the times it no longer called itself a root beer stand but now was billed as a drive-in. Jordahl's Cradle and Tot Shop had moved into Southway in the mid-

1960s, and a couple years after that a book store, Courtney's Books & Things, opened next to the florist.

But I myself was looking at moving. The store at 2111 S. Minnesota Avenue just didn't have enough square footage to accommodate everything I wanted to offer.

About ten blocks south of that location was an area known as South Sioux. One of the roads was 41st Street, which at that time was gravel. But I had a study done and was told it was the next likely location for growth. I can remember that after I had relocated, owners of a car dealership came to me and said, "What do you think about 41st Street?" Frank Weatherwax, owner of a downtown men's clothing store, also came to me for advice before moving to 41st. People were of two minds about my plans: They either thought it was a bad idea or that I was someone to watch.

I was the first of what I call the "new generation," those of us willing to commit to 41st Street. As it turned out, the Western Mall opened farther west on 41st in 1968, a year before my store, but I used my option to buy in 1967 before the mall owners did.

I had looked at staying on Minnesota Avenue but nearer to downtown when I started thinking about moving in 1965. At one point, property on the southeast corner of 33rd Street and Minnesota Avenue came up for sale. I gave my banker a prospectus, but for some reason he didn't move quickly. It had several owners, and for a while served as a center where people enjoyed miniature bowling could play, but the Vern Eide car dealership eventually bought the property.

About that same time is when two men from the National Hardware Retailers Association, of which I was a member, came to Sioux Falls. Howard Mathis and Jim Robish surveyed the area, and they are the ones who advised me to move as close to 41st Street and Minnesota Avenue as I possibly could.

But again, the bank I was dealing with just didn't move quickly. That was when Verlyn Schmidt from Western Bank contacted me. Verlyn said, "Roy, I understand you're looking for some money." I said, "I sure am!" And in about three weeks' time in 1967, I had the money to buy the property on 41st Street, east of a McDonald's Hamburgers owned by Max Pasley.

But even though there was a Kmart a couple blocks north of me, and a few other businesses, my store was going to face 41st Street. I was the new kid on the block, and some people thought I was crazy. "Why are you moving down there?" they would ask. "There's nothing down there."

A man named Ray Brooks owned my future property. His granddaughter, Barbara, now is married to one of South Dakota's two U.S. senators, Tim Johnson. Several buildings needed to be razed before I could build the store, but the Brooks house was not torn down. It was such a nice residence that when I contacted the Brandt moving company, he actually paid me for it. I was told that didn't happen often. Two other structures also had to be removed, one a house owned by a woman named Helen Nordstrom and the other an old barracks moved from the former air base.

I was quite precise in my plans for the store. That goes back to a boyhood interest in architecture. When the land was cleared, I took chalk and outlined the building, even down to where I wanted my counters, just to get a visual idea of how it would look.

Before we built the store on 41st Street, my old boss advised me, "Now, Roy, when you build, try to have all of the planning done so that you don't have any work order changes. Those cost money." So I had that store so well planned, I don't think we changed anything. It was a beautiful store. Whenever anyone complimented me on it, I always responded, "That's the way we planned it."

The groundbreaking was 8:00 a.m. May 12, 1969. An article in the Argus Leader describes it this way: "The new building will have 17,500 square feet of floor space. It will have a two-story elevated effect at the rear. An Indian theme will be used in the interior. There will be entrances from 40th and 41st Streets and a parking lot for 50 vehicles. The present store has a total of 6,000 square feet." It actually had 4,000 square feet.

Gil Haugan Construction Company was the contractor. When the company applied for a building permit, it put the value of my store at

$84,000. The businesses on Minnesota Avenue near 41st Street welcomed me. Max Pasley offered, without me asking, to remove a row of poplar trees that would have blocked my hardware store from motorists' view.

Work had been underway for a only month when tragedy happened. It had rained hard, and puddles formed on the ground. Two construction workers, Craig DeBoer, 19, and James DeLay, 34, were electrocuted when the steel beam they were raising came close to a high-tension wire and arced. The Haugan employees died at the scene.

It was a heartbreaking time for us, my entire family. Kevin, then 11, cried when he heard about the deaths. Our store, begun with such promise, had brought grief to two families. A lawsuit eventually was filed in connection with the deaths. I was told at the time it was the first $1 million suit filed in South Dakota. The suit was against Nyberg's Ace Inc., not me personally, and eventually the store was dropped from the suit. But money is of secondary importance. What matters is people, and two lives were lost. There always has been sadness connected with the new store.

It wasn't the only sorrow I would experience in 1969 and in the months that followed it.

Coming with me to 41st Street was Ernie Kaiser. Ernie had worked with Ed Howlin when he purchased the hardware store at 2111 S. Minnesota Avenue. After Ed had his heart attack, Ernie converted the Marshall Wells hardware to an Ace, doing everything necessary. When Ed decided to sell the store, Ernie evidently didn't have the backing to buy it, or maybe he just didn't want to. But I inherited Ernie with the store and counted myself lucky. My oldest daughter, Jody, worked with Ernie. She remembers him as always happy and with a smile on his face. "A nice, nice man," she says.

By the time we were ready to move to 41st Street and Minnesota Avenue, I managed the store from a small, raised office in the receiving room, and Ernie was the floor manager. He was a good man. At one point, before the move, I told him, "Let me pay for this store, let me say at least it's my store, and at that time I'll take you in as a partner."

That's how it worked out. I retained 75 percent, and he came in at 25 percent. That was in 1967, when we purchased the land on 41st Street for the store. We broke ground in May 1969.

Sadly, Ernie and I were not partners for long. He was diagnosed with leukemia and died in 1972 at the age of 41. That's when I went to his wife, Harriet. I told her that the store was still so new that it was not profitable to where it had increased the assets' value. "But if you let me pay you off over a certain period of time, so much a month with six percent interest, I'll see to it you get every cent that Ernie put into the store," I told her. And I did.

At the same time, I don't always recommend partnerships. To be successful, you have to have someone who thinks exactly the way you do. I was so honest, I wouldn't take a screw or a nail from my own store without paying for it. That's something my old boss, Rudy Erickson, had taught me. He said if you don't, the first thing you know, you'll have depleted your stock, and you won't know where your assets went. Just be honest, he said. Besides, the IRS frowns on it! So as long as I owned the store, I bought the merchandise once, but when I took it from the store I paid for it again.

My old boss, he taught me how to be a darn good businessman. There was no fooling around. Business was business. After I left Hibbing, up through the 1980s, I used to get letters from Rudy offering advice. In 1982, he sent me a copy of an article from Forbes magazine that described how the corner hardware store fought off Sears & Roebuck in the 1950s and home center chains in the 1970s, asking "Is it invincible?" Rudy wrote in his note, "Ace has the larger dealers and is growing faster. It shows what an idea and a plan will do, and the challenge to make it work." It was almost like I was his son.

My father and mother still lived in International Falls. When we lived in Hibbing and the grandkids started arriving, we were able to travel the 100 miles to International Falls frequently to visit my folks. We went there often in the summertime, and Christmas always was spent with Grandma Nyberg or Grandma Dokken on the farm near Kenyon. Kevin received a steam engine one year; we attached it to a Ferris wheel and the steam engine made the Ferris wheel spin. I remember Dad assembling that with Kevin. It was the kind of project that appealed to Dad's creative side. Northern Minnesota was covered with blueberry bushes, and it was during summers at the lake that Dad taught my kids how to pick wild blueberries.

After we moved to Sioux Falls we traveled to the Dokkens' farm more often than we made it up to International Falls. It was only 240 miles to the farm, compared to the 500 miles to my old hometown. I remember traveling one Christmas with unassembled red wagons in the back of our vehicle and returning with the wagons put together.

My parents came to see us every other year or so, often traveling by bus. We went up there when we could. I wish now we'd been able to see my parents more often. But I always had their support in my ventures, and they were proud of the success I was having with my hardware store. They knew it took hard work.

Dad never got to see the new store at 41st Street and Minnesota Avenue. In the summer of 1969, my father was told he had cancer. Rodora and I had gone to the Minneapolis hospital where they were doing surgery that August. When they opened him up, nothing could be done. The doctors came out to see us after only 30 minutes had passed, and we knew it was bad news.

Jody remembers the last time they all saw him was in a visit to the Twin Cities when my folks were staying with Bob and his wife, Char. It was extremely hard for Dad to say goodbye to the grandchildren, Jody says. He knew he would never see them again.

I had rented office space in the Southway Shopping Center where I could isolate myself and concentrate on ordering merchandise and other things that needed to be done for the new store. But between August and October 1969, I took all the papers I was working with, the orders and checklists, up to International Falls as often as possible. I did my work on a card table in the living room. When my father felt up to coming out of his bedroom, we could visit. That's the way I spent my time with my dad. He died October 23, 1969. I wish he could have seen the seventy-foot-tall sign and his name on the store in eight-foot neon flashing letters: Nyberg's Ace Hardware.

That sign created a brief furor. Because everybody thought I was crazy to move to 41st Street, I wanted to make a bold statement. I had George Meinke of Pride Neon come to the site. Using a boom, he dangled a large letter in the air. I went up to my competitor at 35th Street and Minnesota Avenue, Lewis Drug Store, to see if I could see the letter. When it was high enough, I told George to stop. That's why the sign still today is 70 feet tall. Originally it was installed on the store's west side because there was a parking lot between the store and property line.

As a result of my sign, Sioux Falls' city fathers created an ordinance saying no signs could be that tall in the future. I don't know what their objection to it was. It wasn't in any flight path. But, man, did I use that sign. Our slogan was "It's all under the tall sign at 41st Street and Minnesota Avenue." Sometimes a little controversy can be good for business, if you use it right as a marketing tool.

The store opened on September 7, 1969. I have the receipt from the first sale at 7:53 a.m. for $6.25 to a former neighbor, John Wiedmeier, who had moved to Billings, Montana. He sent the cash so he could be the first customer. The grand opening was scheduled for five weeks later, from November 13th to 15th.

It was a successful launch. You would think I would have gone through enough in 1969 that I would be content with what I had. But I have a letter dated November 19, 1969, from Carl Bicking, then vice-president with Ace Hardware. Another Ace representative had reported that my tentative plans "are to open another store or two and one possibility is Fargo, North Dakota." Bicking cautioned me that an Ace franchise already was operating in Fargo, but he added, "On the other hand your selection of Sioux City would seem to be wiser."

I don't remember it now, but apparently I had been talking big, perhaps inspired by the euphoria that comes along with seeing a project successfully completed. Carl Bicking also suggested that I might want to consider opening a second store in Sioux Falls.

As it turns out, that is what eventually happened, and then some. But it was my son, Kevin, who made that come about.

A Scout is...reverent and thrifty

Chapter 14
CHANGING WITH THE TIMES

It wasn't just Sioux Falls retailers who were watching the opening of Nyberg's Ace Hardware in the fall of 1969. People were taking note nationally, too. Hardware Trade, a magazine for hardware retailers, opened a story about the new store with a quote from the National Retail Hardware Association: "As modern and innovative as any hardware store west of Chicago and east of the coastal states."

Hardware stores had two images to battle for too many years: 1) that they were high-priced, and 2) that they were dim, dusty places, suitable only for men.

My new store set out to dispel both of those myths. An article in the January 1970 Hardware News & Views newsletter, published by the Minnesota-Dakotas Retail Hardware Association, described this scene:

> "They were young mothers – between 24 and 30, and their children were in school. Two housewives, out for an afternoon of shopping. They walked into the brightly lighted store after parking their car in the convenient free parking lot right in front of the store.
>
> "It was 'Grand Opening' and the first thing they did was sign up for free prizes that were to be given away. They then reached for a handy shopping cart, TOOK OFF THEIR COATS, and put them in the bottom of the cart and began their shopping tour of the store!

"Was this the local supermarket? Or the Discount store? No – it was the brand new, local hardware store – the hardware store of the 1970s, if you please! 'And they took off their coats and began to shop!'"

That incident is true. It happened at Nyberg's Ace Hardware during our grand opening.

My goal from the beginning had been to create a store that had something for everyone. So the new location included two large departments: giftwares and housewares.

From the beginning, I had wanted a store that was unique. The interior carried a Native American theme with pictures of famous Indian chiefs. Arrowheads quarried from native rock at Pipestone, Minnesota, tipped the rods that held sign banners.

I had a tree oasis installed where people could rest on benches. We even put in an antique pot-bellied stove as a tribute to the stoves that once upon a time always were found in hardware stores and where male customers gathered.

But nostalgia didn't get in the way of my determination to make this the most modern store possible. And to bring in women.

Helping me in that goal was Elmer Mick, who operated his own store in Worthington, Minnesota. We met because smaller stores often joined together to make bulk purchases, saving money that way. I worked frequently with Elmer and Croz Demaray, who operated the Pipestone Ace Hardware. We'd get together some evening and say, I have to have garbage cans, or I have to have ladders, or we were buying toys for Christmas. So we'd determine the quantity each man wanted, and someone would bring in one company, and another guy would bring in another company. We'd get together over at Luverne, Minnesota, a convenient meeting place, with our station wagons and shuffle merchandise around.

Elmer and his wife, Doris, were big in housewares, and Doris did a great job in buying for the women's market. I convinced Elmer to come over here for three days a week. I hired him to run housewares and be the merchandiser. He was with me before Ernie Kaiser, my partner in the new store, died, but Elmer became even more important after Ernie's death in 1971. When Doris and Elmer went to market and bought for themselves, they also were buying for me.

Having a giftwares department was unusual for an Ace store, but I thought it was essential. Elmer and Doris did the buying for that department, too. Between Akers Gifts & Collectibles, located north of us on Minnesota Avenue, and my store, we probably had the finest giftwares departments in Sioux Falls. It was a successful department for years, but sales began dwindling about the time country crafts became so popular. People would make their own items and sell them at church bazaars and so forth. The Ace giftwares department and Akers both are gone now.

Now, we were also big in sporting goods. Again, we were innovators. Every fall we would offer what was called a family hunters stag. We would have renowned sportsmen come here and demonstrate shooting or archery. We invited wildlife artists. We would set up the back room so we could have Daisy BB gun shoots for children and stress gun safety, something that has been important to me since my days in Hibbing.

I sold Lowell Hansen Jr., the former South Dakota lieutenant governor, his first gun, and he became quite the sportsman. We sold a lot of guns before Scheels came to town. I was familiar with the Scheels store because they were basically hardware people up in Fargo.

I always have taken the position that I did not want to get too involved in any one department to the detriment of the others. First and foremost, I wanted to be darn sure we were known for hardware and that sort of thing. So when Scheels began cutting into our gun sales, I didn't worry too much. We were selling a lot of hunting clothing and tents and sleeping bags, and we still do.

It's just the nature of competition. When you're in business, you take advantage. I'm not saying you take advantage of your competition, but you take advantage of the situation. If something new is coming out and you take advantage of that, you're going to be the forerunner. After we moved to the new store, I had salesmen come to me wanting me to sell their products. I would say, "Okay, I'll take on your line, and I can make your manufacturer a household name here in Sioux Falls. But just bear with me. It takes time."

Sometimes they were patient, sometimes they weren't. And I could get bull-headed. We were selling Eclipse lawn mowers – a LOT of Eclipse lawn mowers – when Snapper asked me to start carrying their lawnmower line. I wasn't too anxious to do it, but I did. And we were successful. But that's when Snapper decided if one store carrying our line is good, two or three would be better.

They came to me and said they would like to have another dealer in town. I said I don't mind as long as you come to me, and I'll let you know if I want them to be a competitor. Because I know my competitors enough to know if they would hold the price. But they didn't do that; they took on somebody who would play games. The next year the fellow came up and said, "I'm here to get the spring order." I said, "I'm no longer a Snapper dealer." He said, "Oh, yes, you are." I said, "No, I'm no longer a Snapper dealer." And I wasn't. I quit. That's how bull-headed I was. And here I had sold 200 the year before.

But what I'm saying is, you have to be willing to change. As I look back at my competitors who no longer are in existence, I have to say they probably failed because they didn't have enough foresight. And being *involved* with state, regional and national hardware associations also gave me good instincts.

That doesn't mean I didn't encounter problems. New stores and store expansions usually are not profitable for two to three years. About 1972, three years after I moved the store to 41st and Minnesota, I received a call from my banker. He told me, "Roy, you go back to the store and redo your budget and tell me how you're going to scale down expenses to the income you've got. And if you can't do it by eight o'clock tomorrow morning, you might as well close your doors."

We hadn't turned a profit for a while, and the banker had become alarmed. Maybe the sales hadn't come in as fast as I had expected, or maybe I just wasn't watching expenses vs. income as closely as I should have been.

So Elmer Mick and I sat down and reworked the budget. I took a salary cut and cut back on some other expenses, and the rest is history. We had ups and downs over the years, but nothing close to that. It was just a simple law of business that I needed to follow: You've got to have more money coming in than you're spending

From the beginning, it seemed like we were constantly expanding. A car wash was operating next to me, and the owner wanted to sell the property. I bought it and tried running the car wash for a while, but it was a nuisance. I wanted to sell it, and I couldn't find anybody to buy the darned thing. So I bought three houses on Minnesota Avenue, across from the Minnehaha County Courthouse, and two more on Dakota Avenue because they sold as a package. I was going to tear down the Minnesota Avenue houses and put the car wash there. Just about the time we were going to do that, a fellow came along and offered us $10,000 for the car wash. He took it up to North Cliff Avenue, and it sat in his yard for years. I don't know if he ever put the thing back together.

But with the car wash gone, I had room next to my store. We built a freestanding building at the far-west property line to house lawn and garden equipment in the spring, summer and fall and toys before Christmas. Right along our remaining property line, we fenced that in and built kiosks for shovels, rakes and fertilizer.

It became obvious that 17,500 square feet, which had seemed so large when I envisioned the new store, wasn't going to be enough room. We ended up having two major expansions. After a groundbreaking on August 9, 1977, the Lawn & Garden Center opened in 1978. That expanded total retail space to 26,000 square feet with 3,000 square feet in offices and warehouse. Our grand opening began August 29, 1978, and continued through September.

Max Pasley, who owned the McDonald's to our west, was a good neighbor. Together the two of us resolved several issues that others might have taken to court. For example, once Max put a cold-storage freezer right on our property line. In fact, it ended up being a foot over the line onto my property. But rather than make a big issue of it, when it came time to add onto our building, we just made a one-foot jog in the plans. You can see it if you look at our west wall.

In 1984, it was time to give the store a new look. By that time, Kevin was the store manager, and he supervised the remodeling.

In an article in the April 29, 1984, Argus Leader, I remembered once again my old partner, Ernie Kaiser. He had a personality and charisma that I envied, and I wondered how many stores we might have opened had he lived and the partnership gone on for decades. The story notes, "But the possibility of any new stores now rests with the new generation."

All four of my children grew up around the hardware store, as have all but the youngest of the nine grandchildren. We were fortunate that the kids showed an interest in the family business and that someone wanted to take it over.

I knew it was not that way for everyone.

A Scout is...helpful and courteous

Chapter 15
STATE AND NATIONAL INVOLVEMENT

I want to share something that I've been using in speeches for well over 30 years:

> "The beginning and the end. Everything comes from the earth. It's either mined, or it's grown. Nothing happens until something is consumed which is generally purchased on the main streets of our cities and towns. Now, if you're not a part of the beginning or the end (meaning farming, mining and main street), it is in your best interest to help keep the beginning and end healthy and happy. The manufacturer, fabricator, insurance industry, transportation, warehouses, distributors, advertising medias and on and on all depend on the productivity of the man of the earth and main street."

I have shared those thoughts in a variety of situations, most notably during two White House Conferences on Small Business in the 1980s. The first time I attended the conference, I had been appointed by Larry Pressler, a Republican who served South Dakota for 18 years, beginning in 1979. The second time, I had to run as a candidate, and I used "the beginning and the end" statement on my campaign literature.

As the owner of a small business, I recognized early on the importance of taking an active role in various associations. Even a small businessman can be mighty if he bands together with others in similar situations.

In May 1988, I was featured in Hardware Merchandiser magazine. The headline for the story was one that made me proud: "A Voice for the Little Guy."

At that point, I was president of the National Retail Hardware Association. It was the culmination of an *involvement* that had begun in 1961 when I first was elected to the South Dakota Retail Hardware Association. I had become a member of the SDRHA probably within my first year of moving to Sioux Falls. Members used to have the annual meeting at the Coliseum. The man who got me *involved*, Harris Benson, ran a hardware store at Chester and also served as the SDRHA secretary, the top person.

In 1967, I became president of the SDRHA. During that period I spearheaded the merger of the South Dakota group into what is now the Minnesota-Dakotas Retail Hardware Association. It was merge or die. Small towns were losing their hardware stores. And we don't have a lot of large cities in this state. As the stores closed, our membership dwindled. You can't support a secretary and supply him with what he needs if you don't have an adequate budget based on membership dues.

At the same time, North Dakota also was having similar problems. The Minnesota group voted to accept its neighbors to the west, and that's how the Minnesota-Dakotas Retail Hardware Association came about.

During the period between the time Harris Benson left as secretary and we merged with the Minnesota group, the National Retail Hardware Association took us under its wing. Dwayne Laws, a Kentucky native, would come to South Dakota and help keep us alive.

While he was here, he picked up on something I'd been sharing with my employees for several years and turned it into an educational film called "Three Pennies."

The premise is simple: Demonstrate in an easy-to-understand way how difficult it can be to make a profit.

I would stack up 100 pennies and then begin by saying, "I'm going to show you just how many pennies are left over each time we get a dollar from a customer." First: Take away 60 pennies. What's that for?

Well, when the merchandise comes in the back door, I have to pay for it. That costs sixty cents of every dollar.

Next, I would have an employee take two cents away. That pays for the electricity and other utilities. I'd say, take three cents away for advertising. The employee would do that, and thirty-five cents would remain on the table. The employees might think that was it, but I'd say, "Don't you want to be paid?" So another twenty cents would be taken away. Before paying income taxes, there would be only three cents left. It was a good, visual demonstration of how hard it is for a retailer to make a profit.

I shared that example once again this year when I met with many members of the South Dakota Legislature when Kevin and I were honored as the South Dakota Retailers Association 2010 Retailer of the Year Award. It impressed several people. I don't think customers realize main street businessmen don't keep as much money as they think we do.

I continued on the MDRHA board until 1973, serving as president in 1971-1972. We didn't have any major problems during my tenure, except about ten minutes after I received the gavel as president the executive director resigned.

That wasn't the only state association board that kept me busy. I also became *involved* with the South Dakota Retailers Association. That group also went through a rocky period. In fact, it splintered at one point, and I played a role in bringing it back into existence.

Keep in mind, members of the SDRA included everything from small businesses to large stores such as Sears & Roebuck, J.C. Penney and Montgomery Ward. We wanted to buy a property for our headquarters that was north of the Capitol building in Pierre. It was an old filling station. But the members from "the majors," the larger stores, balked. They feared the underground gas tanks would cause problems down the road.

Now, this assumption always has irritated me: When someone manages a large store, people assume that person is smarter or has a better business sense or is more capable than a small businessman. A college degree isn't always a sign of common sense. So when we decided to go ahead and buy the property, "the majors" said they were leaving the association. Our executive director went with them.

We hired a new executive director and proceeded with our plans to buy the filling station. But our former executive director had made a mistake. He turned the odometer back on his vehicle and was caught. We told our new executive secretary to forget about it. I liked the old director, and I'm a big believer in second chances. He had just done something foolish. But our new director pursued it, and the former director was prosecuted.

A couple of years later, "the majors" came back to the SDRA. They hadn't had an easy time of it after they struck out on their own. So the executive director and I met with them in Sioux Falls, and they agreed to rejoin us. In the meantime, we had built an office on the filling station property, and we've never had a problem with it.

It also was difficult a few years earlier when the then-executive secretary wanted to move the headquarters from Pierre to Sioux Falls. He had personal reasons for doing so. But I wouldn't go along with that. I insisted it had to remain in Pierre, the center of the state.

I took a break from hardware association boards for a couple of years, from 1973 until 1977 when I was elected to the National Retail Hardware Association board. That group has changed its name to North American Retail Hardware Association to better acknowledge its members north and south of the United States, but the initials remain the same, NRHA.

When I joined the NRHA board, one of the first things I did was call my old boss Rudy Erickson, who still lived in International Falls, and ask for his advice. I always have had a deep admiration for the man and valued what he taught me. I wanted to know what ideas he had for the NRHA.

Rudy was about to retire from his hardware and furniture stores, but he still maintained an active interest in the industry. He had been *involved* with Ace Hardware for about 40 years.

According to a history of Ace, five hardware store owners joined to form a purchasing and advertising partnership in the Chicago area in 1924. Together, they negotiated lower prices on merchandise purchased from wholesalers. The Ace name was adopted in 1927, taken from the ace fighter pilots in World War I who could overcome all odds. Ace quickly evolved into a wholesaling organization. It would buy directly from manufacturers and store merchandise in its own warehouse. "Middlemen" wholesalers were eliminated, and Ace members had a competitive edge among other hardware stores.

Richard "Dick" Hesse, one of the five original founders, became Ace's president in 1930. When Dick retired in late 1973, he sold Ace to its member-dealers, thereby forming a dealer-owned hardware cooperative. Now, several years before Dick retired, Rudy had suggested that very same thing, and Dick took it badly. Dick was domineering; in fact, he reminded me of Napoleon both in size and attitude. He didn't like any signs of independence from the dealers. He didn't like it when Ace store owners shopped around, trying to find a better price so we could buy something for less. You WILL buy from Ace, was Dick's attitude, and you WILL have Ace paint, you WILL have an Ace sign.

My old boss Rudy was good friends with Gunnard Linquist, one of Ace's officers. Linquist would come up to International Falls to fish with Rudy. So when Rudy and Linquist suggested, "Dick, why don't you sell Ace Hardware to the dealers for fifty cents on the dollar?," that made Dick Hesse unhappy. His longtime friendship with Rudy came to an end. But upon Dick's retirement that's exactly what ultimately happened, and member-dealers did buy Ace Hardware at fifty cents on the dollar.

I still respected and admired my old boss. So I listened when Rudy expressed his concern about the continuity of the independent or family-owned hardware store. I not only listened, I brought it up to the NRHA board.

As a result, the NRHA's Mueller Foundation commissioned a study to look at the problems and possible solutions to keeping family-owned hardware stores and home centers continuing. The Mueller Foundation, named after Russell Mueller who had been the NRHA's managing director from 1952 through 1967, was created to conduct research and plan educational activities for the improvement of hardware retailing.

The two-year research project, undertaken by Fred A. Tillman and Jack Rice, resulted in a 325-page book titled, "Who's Next Please?: A Strategy for Planning the Succession and Perpetuation of the Family Owned Hardware Store or Home Center." The book has proven to be amazingly helpful to countless families and independent small businesses as they prepared to transfer ownership to a family member or some other successor.

Through my *experience* as a member of hardware associations, I had witnessed the sadness that followed when a family-owned business had failed to plan for the future and as a result lost that business. I am immensely pleased to have played a role in averting such tragedies.

"Who's Next Please?" covered many areas, including why it's important to do more than put together a no-frills will when it comes to continuing a business; how to plan for retirement through things such as IRAs and Social Security; and how to choose a successor to a family business, whether it's a family member or someone from outside.

The Nyberg family, in fact, was featured in the book's epilogue. Our name was changed to Johnson, but we were used as an example of what to do in ensuring a family succession. I'll share more about that later.

During my years on the NRHA, I saw other state associations struggle as membership numbers dropped, just as had happened in South Dakota. Other mergers, such as Washington and Oregon joining with California, were happening with regularity. When I went on the board, there were 25 or 30 secretaries, or association leaders, who would come to the NRHA headquarters twice a year. But the numbers continued to drop.

We were at an executive meeting in Florida when I made the comment that someday the NRHA, with its main office in Indianapolis, would have to become the parent organization for many of these states. That is exactly what happened. As this is written, there are only two state organizations left. One of those is the MDRHA, which now also includes Wisconsin.

Because of my *involvement* with the hardware associations, the Nyberg family was *exposed* to many different places and cultures. It could be a heady experience. In our industry, I have been up there at the top. When we had our conventions, Rodora and I had the presidential suites with the white grand pianos. I was vice president when we went to Washington, D.C. The year I was president, we had our national convention in Orlando. I said the one thing I'd like to do with the board of directors, I'd like to see the basement, I want to go underground at Disney World. Not too many people have done that, but we did. We went in that whole complex, seeing people run around in their costumes, ready to go upstairs and entertain the visitors. I'm just sharing this because you talk about this *environment, involvement, exposure*, I've been there.

My *involvement* with the NRHA also took Rodora and me to other countries. I've been at The Hague in Holland, I've gone to Ottawa, Canada, and Stockholm, Sweden. In Stockholm, Rodora and I stayed on the same hotel floor the same day as Nancy Reagan. I've got pictures of her. In Montreaux, Switzerland, everyone who attended received a watch, one that probably cost only $10. It's 20 years old now, and it's needed only two batteries. I wear it as a reminder of what I've *experienced*.

I admit, there were disappointments along the way. I was the first NRHA president who was not invited to the White House's Rose Garden. I think only one NRHA president has been invited there in the twenty-plus years since.

In Stockholm, I was scheduled to speak at the international Ironmongers convention – their name for hardware stores – and I had my speech all written. I always wrote my own speeches. But first it was decided that the NRHA wouldn't pay for my trip over there, so I did. Then someone else in the organization took my slot when it came time to give the speech. That was a disappointment on many levels, but especially since my dad had come from Sweden. It would have meant a lot to be to be the keynote speaker at a convention in my dad's home country.

If there have been disappointments in my life, they came when I ran up against what I call hot-doggers, those who demand the spotlight and the glory. I'm not a hot-dogger. I've been there, done that, but I don't play games. I'm a fair person.

And sentimental. That's the word Rodora uses to describe me. It's true: I've been known to cry when Miss America is crowned. Band competitions are sure to make me well up with tears, or when someone receives an award. My family teases me about it. But there's nothing wrong with letting your emotions show. And one emotion I'm quick to display is pride in my family.

To help other people at all times

Chapter 16
A FAMILY OF SIX

Rodora and I learned about parenting from our own parents, and we were fortunate to have good role models. But on our own, we decided to stress something else to Jody, Nancy, Kevin and Marin: Be different! Be different! They are, too. Our four children listened carefully to that advice!

Despite working hard to make the hardware store a success, I missed only one parent-teacher conference and never failed to attend a recital, play or concert performance. Of course, our kids weren't as involved in extracurricular activities as our grandchildren are today. Today, my older kids say I was strict. Nancy remembers being grounded for what the kids viewed as small infractions such as not turning out the lights when they left a room. In fact, Jody says she was "grounded like a DC-10." Marin, on the other hand, has no memory of ever being grounded. But then, her siblings call her the perfect child. Marin says she never was grounded because she had no siblings around so there was no one with whom to quarrel!

During my years as a father with a young family, I sometimes found myself drawing on past experiences to guide my children. One such instance occurred when Kevin was about 13 years old. He was good friends with Rich Menzel, the son of my buddy Lew Menzel, despite the fact there was more than three years' difference in age. It was close to the age gap between my younger brother Bob and I.

Rich idolized Kevin. One night Lew and I took the boys to a basketball game. Rich and Kevin were sitting in the front row, while Lew and I had seats higher in the stands. I glanced down at one point in the game and saw Rich sitting by himself, head in his hands, extremely downcast. Evidently Kevin, engrossed with friends who were his own age, had left Rich alone, and Rich was near tears at the rejection.

When Kevin and I arrived home after the game, Kevin told me what happened. As an adult, I had come to realize how much my younger brother looked up to me and what an impact my own actions had on Bob. So I told Kevin, "It takes a lifetime to build a friendship, but it only takes a few seconds to tear it down." (That is true of any relationship.) I suggested, but did not demand, that he apologize to Rich. Kevin followed my advice. To this day, Kevin knows that his actions can hurt someone else's feeling. If he has a customer that for some reason is unhappy, for example, Kevin will send them a gift certificate to try to smooth things over. It was an early lesson in relationships that he has never forgotten.

While my twenty-five-year involvement with organizations such as the National Retail Hardware Association could have taken me away from the family, instead we turned the conventions into a time to be together. The NRHA always conducted its conventions in major metropolitan areas such as Boston, New York City, Orlando, San Diego, Portland, Denver and Montreal, Canada. Nancy, Kevin and Marin had visited all of the lower 48 states by the time they graduated from high school.

In the beginning, we hitched a fourteen-foot Forester trailer to our vehicle and pulled that, sleeping in the trailer at night. We towed that trailer up to Montreal, and I even drove it through Times Square in New York City. We were like gypsies with our trailer. Later we traveled by motor home.

We would spend a week or ten days on the road, and the conventions always had activities planned for the participants' children. Rodora and I would look for other activities for them, too. Whenever possible, we would take in professional theater productions. The one I remember most vividly is "The Flower Drum Song," a Rodgers & Hammerstein musical that includes the song "I Enjoy Being a Girl."

We bought the album, and Jody, Nancy and Kevin would reenact the musical, sitting in front of the stereo and pretending they were the characters. Again, *environment, exposure* and *involvement* played a strong role in their upbringing.

We raised good kids, although some people probably wouldn't think it was a particularly religious home. We didn't sit down and read the Bible together, but Rodora and I did try to inspire the kids to live a righteous life.

All four kids worked at the store at some time in their lives, whether as youngsters, in high school or as adults. Jody and Kevin can remember working there when they were nine years old, dusting shelves and sorting screws that customers had jumbled up, putting them back in the proper bins. Jody recalls walking to the Minnesota Avenue store from our rental house on Duluth Avenue. We would walk across the A&W root beer stand parking lot, and she never failed to find ten or fifteen cents in spilled change.

Jody, our oldest, worked for me for ten years. That includes during high school and for several years after her freshman year at Augustana College in Sioux Falls. She created the rules and regulations we used as an employee handbook and organized the store in that regard. She worked full time for me after one year of college. Jody had come to me that spring and said, "Dad, if you want to send me to Augie, you can do that, but you're just going to be wasting your money." She had been a straight-A student at Lincoln High School, but she just did not want college. I told her, okay, come work at the store, and I will teach you the hardware business.

Jody says that was when the store was struggling financially. It was a tense time, and Rodora had told her everyone needed to work to make the store a success. Jody didn't think she could juggle college and a full-time job and do either one well. But she says she never regretted the choice she made, and not having a college degree has never stopped her from being successful.

After working at the store and living in her own apartment until she was 23, Jody moved to Minneapolis where, as I have said, she eventually became the first woman store manager for Warner Hardware. Rodora describes Jody as very self-confident, and some of that comes from being a pioneer.

Jody later moved to Farwell, Ozmun, Kirk & Company in St. Paul, commonly known as FOK, where she became the buyer for electrical devices, switch plates, lights and so forth. They promoted her to housewares and Christmas items, and she was very good at that position. It was at FOK that Jody met her future husband, Bob Rasmussen, and they were married on May 3, 1980. Jody later joined Farberware where she worked alongside Julia Child, the famous chef, almost ten times when Child had national cooking shows with Farberware. Jody and Bob now live in Asheville, North Carolina, where she is a buyer for the historic Biltmore, the largest home in the United States.

Nancy, our second daughter, really didn't come to work at the hardware store until she was an adult. As the second child, I think she wanted to follow her own path. Nancy always will stick up for herself and for what she wants but not in a combative way. She is very lovable, and she's the one who never forgets birthdays and anniversaries. She likes to honor those occasions with personal gifts. It's not necessary, but it makes people feel special. Nancy has crocheted 70 afghans for family and friends over the years. She's also the communicator, the one who keeps in touch with far-away relatives and friends.

After high school, she worked as a checker at Sunshine Grocery Store, not in the hardware store. She used the money she had earned to buy herself a car, a 1972 silver-blue AMC Gremlin with blue-jean interior. Nancy was so proud of having her own car at a time when her friends from high school were in college.

Later Nancy became a teller at Union Bank & Trust in downtown Sioux Falls where her former co-workers still ask me about her. As an adult, she came to work in the store office, handling the purchase journal and payroll. But again, I was not her direct supervisor.

Nancy was the first of our children to bring an in-law into the family, marrying Rick Swanson Jr. on September 18, 1976. After their children were born, Nancy worked on the hardware store's books at home. That allowed her to be there with the children until they were old enough for her to work at the store full time.

Rodora describes Nancy as caring and generous. With her outgoing personality, she will strike up friendly conversations with complete strangers. We have often teased her over the years that after she meets someone for the first time they are now on her extensive Christmas card list. She may have inherited this gene from me as I also get accused of turning a quick errand into a lengthy affair by stopping to talk to anyone I meet.

Today she works with Communication Service for the Deaf here in Sioux Falls as a communicator assistant. In 2009 she underwent chemotherapy for breast cancer. It was a difficult time for Rodora and me watching our child suffer. But Nancy maintained a positive attitude. A year later, to our great shock, Nancy learned her breast cancer had returned. But she has pledged to put on her "boxing gloves" and defeat the disease once again.

Rick works as a buyer for the lawn and garden and sporting goods departments for all four stores. Nancy and Rick have three daughters, Laura, Caryn and Jennifer. Caryn is the first of our grandchildren to marry; we'll have another wedding in 2011 when granddaughter Laura is married.

When Nancy's first two children were born, Rodora and I were out of town. We didn't expect to be gone for Laura's birth, but she came six weeks early. I never witnessed my own children's births. Even when Marin was born, once again I was in the waiting room because it still was unusual for a father to witness the delivery. I always felt I missed something. When Nancy was expecting a third time, she asked if I wanted to watch her give birth, and I said yes. But Nancy went into labor just when I was supposed to leave town for a trip. I left the delivery room to make phone arrangements to change my flight – and Jennifer arrived so quickly I missed the actual birth. But I did get to cut the umbilical cord, and I was the first one to hold her.

I have a note Kevin wrote to me just before the grand opening of the new store at 41st Street and Minnesota Avenue. It says:

"Dad!
  1) Congratulations
  2) Can I have a ride to school tomorrow.

3) Should I wear my suit to the store tomorrow
4) Thanks for everything tonite
5) Good luck in store
6) Goodnite

                Kevin Nyberg future owner of Ace 2
                    (not same building too small)."

At that point, Kevin already had been working in the store for three years. He would take all the bolts or nails from their bins and vacuum out the dust, then replace them. It's a job that hasn't been done since. He also would make sure any misplaced bolts and nails were in the proper bins.

But despite his confident prediction as a twelve-year-old, Kevin was fired from his job at the store when he was in high school. I didn't fire him! I was never his boss. But his attitude briefly had turned defiant, and either Herb Lohnes or Elmer Mick fired him. It didn't last long, probably only a couple weeks until his attitude changed.

Kevin turned down two opportunities to join me at the store before eventually deciding it was where he wanted to be. After graduating from Lincoln High School and before starting at Augustana College, he spent a summer interning with U.S. Senator Larry Pressler in Washington, D.C. When he returned, he continued to work on Pressler's staff. He spent so much time at that his course work at Augustana suffered.

When Kevin was in Washington, D.C., he became good friends with the lobbyist for the National Retail Hardware Association, my pal Shelly London. When Kevin finished college with majors in political science and business administration, he thought he might be interested in the law as a profession, so he returned to Washington, D.C.

But he didn't like reading briefs and spending his time in a law library. He missed South Dakota, its climate and its hunting opportunities. So he asked to come back and work with me. I am extremely pleased with all my kids, and I don't like to single out Kevin. But without a doubt, Kevin has become a very capable businessman. I've have seen a lot of sons take over their dad's business and not go anywhere with it. Kevin is the one who added three stores. I had one store, he's got four.

Kevin married Linda Samuelson on February 15, 1986. Linda works as a medical technologist at Sanford Health. They have four children: Kelly, Erik and twins, Kirsten and Karmen. Erik followed in his father's footsteps by also becoming editor of the Lincoln Statesman. They are the only father-son team of editors in the high school's forty-five-year history.

Marin, our youngest, is the only one of the four to be born in Sioux Falls. I thought our family was complete, but with the first three growing older – the girls were teenagers – and me caught up in making the store a success, Rodora decided to expand our family. She would see women with babies at the grocery store, and it bothered her. Rodora says now that it was her idea, yet finding out she was pregnant came as a big surprise. She remembers telling the doctor, "You can't get pregnant just looking at each other."

Marin was born July 12, 1966. Rodora and I announced her pregnancy at Christmas by giving the three kids one last package to open. Inside was a baby's Christmas stocking. Jody remembers being embarrassed when she found out her mother was pregnant, but when Marin arrived, Jody and Nancy were excited to have a little sister. Kevin, however, had counted on a brother to whom he could give his Tonka trucks.

Marin is the most low-key of our children. I remember going to a parent-teacher conference when she was a student at Patrick Henry Junior High and telling a teacher I was worried because Marin didn't seem to be outgoing. The teacher politely said, "Don't you worry about Marin. When Marin says something, she's got something to say." To this day that's the way Marin is.

In high school Marin was thinking about teaching autistic children. But Rodora and I took her to an intensive aptitude-testing program at Tulsa, Oklahoma, and she was advised against that profession. The experts told her she was the type of person who needed to see results, and that wouldn't happen quickly with autistic children. The testers also noted her skills in being able to read something once and recall it perfectly.

Marin began working at the hardware store the year she graduated from Augustana College. She and a local TV personality would tape television commercials. In one advertisement, she played a bride, and she needed to list 10 or 12 products that showed our store had items suitable for wedding gifts for a new couple's home. Marin read the script once and nailed the commercial the first time. The testers were right. Today, as advertising and public relations director, Marin is in charge of preparing our circulars, handling promotions at the store, and writing and recording television and radio commercials. Marin performed in talent shows and musicals from elementary school through college. Her love of performing is reflected in her work today.

Marin married Bruce Huber on October 10, 1992. He is the manager of the store's warehouse. Bruce's hobby is weight-lifting, and he has set the South Dakota record for his age class. He also placed second in the world in the 242-pound weight class, masters division, at a meet in Las Vegas.

Marin and Bruce have two daughters, Camryn and Allison. Marin loves music, and she says when she thinks of her childhood she remembers records were always playing at home, and we'd sing in the car. When she was a girl, Marin balked at going on a trip to Nashville, but she came back with a love for country music. Singer Marie Osmond became Marin's idol.

Nancy says we are generous grandparents. It is a pleasure to be able to help our grandchildren and others. When Laura was in middle school, she was *involved* in a Future Problem Solving program that meant the participants needed to travel to a competition. Because of a shortage of funds, one child was going to have to stay home. When I heard that, I made an anonymous donation so everyone could go. (I guess it's not anonymous anymore!)

Rodora stayed home while the children were small. She has been the backbone of our family, the one who was always there. Having her at home when the kids were small was what we both wanted. I had grown up knowing Mother would be home when school let out. I always walked in the house's back door and hollered out, "Mom!"

"Yeah?" she'd answer. "Just wanted to know if you were home," I'd reply.

When we lived in Hibbing and I traveled to trade shows, Rodora would remain home with the children. She says I would call home and say, "Oh, I just finished a big steak dinner at such-and-such hotel," and she would reply, "Well, that's good. WE had tomato soup in the can." Or toasted cheese sandwiches. Or liver or something. But she would be good-natured about it.

Rodora did start working in the store after Marin was in school, but she'd be at home when the kids finished classes. She worked in the receiving area for years, never on the sales floor. Our family always jokes, "Don't give Mother the change box when it comes to a rummage sale because she can never make change."

Freight would come in during the morning, and her work generally was done by afternoon. She liked not having to dress up to go to work, just wear boots that kept her feet warm. In pre-computer days, Rodora would keep track of defective merchandise, then she would come to the manufacturers' shows with me and go from booth to booth to get credit for those products.

I didn't supervise Rodora at work. For all practical purposes, she was the boss in the receiving room. I think her co-workers enjoyed her company because Rodora took her job seriously but also knew how to have fun doing it. After I retired, she continued working for a few more years.

She asked me recently if she ever got paid. If she didn't, I owe her a lot of money! But I'm sure she did. We wanted to make sure she would receive Social Security benefits in her own name if something happened to me.

For a short time, my mother lived with us. After my dad's death in 1969, she had remained in International Falls, living in the house they had shared on 9th Avenue with raspberry bushes in the backyard. She remained active for several years, but then her younger brother, John, who had retired from his position in Washington, D.C., returned to International Falls and helped her handle her finances, reported she was unable to take care of herself anymore.

Mother moved into an apartment for senior citizens. I think now that was a mistake. Away from familiar surroundings, she became more confused, and at some point that confusion was diagnosed as Alzheimer's disease. The doctors didn't think she should be alone so she came to live with my family in Sioux Falls. We set up a bedroom for her in our house's lower level.

Alzheimer's is a tragic disease, robbing a person of their memories and their ability to do even the simplest of tasks. Rodora would be working at the hardware store when my mother would call her in a panic because water was flooding from the faucet. Rodora would rush home, only to find that all she needed to do was turn off the tap. But there were humorous times, too. Mother would fuss about the care she was getting, saying that for the money she paid she deserved better treatment from her caregivers. Rodora would reply, good-naturedly, "Well, Grandma, the help doesn't come very cheap here."

After several months, my mother's care at home became too much for us. Rodora needed to get up several times every night because Mother would wrinkle the sheets and blankets so badly she couldn't sleep and needed help straightening them. Mother moved to a Good Samaritan Center for several months, and on March 15, 1983, she died of kidney failure in a Sioux Falls hospital.

No matter your age, when you have lost both of your parents, it is a difficult time. You now take over as the oldest generation. I was a month short of my 57th birthday.

With my mother's death, I proposed making some changes to the family property at Rainy Lake, installing a building for showers so we didn't have to go into town or use the lake. My brother, Bob, wasn't interested so I offered to sell my half-share to him, and Bob accepted. But Rodora and I wanted a place of our own where we could go. Ever since our honeymoon, we had enjoyed the Black Hills and had vacationed there with the children.

Grandpa and Grandma Dokken, Rodora's parents, also had died, leaving her 80 acres of prime Goodhue County farmland. She sold that land and with that money and my inheritance from my folks, we set out to buy a parcel of land in the Black Hills. We think our parents would be proud that they had helped us achieve a dream.

Sven Froiland, a biology professor at Augustana College, suggested we buy land next to his. I was tempted to do that, but when Kevin looked at the property, he said we needed a place with more trees. He pointed out another nearby lot, which adjoined Sven's, and we ended up buying 20 acres south of his property in 1987.

In 1988 a road to our property was built, and we brought in electricity. We lived in our motor home for two summers, but then I drew the plans for a cabin. Our builder liked it so much he ended up using it for several other homes in the area. We call our place The Lazy Rs for Rodora and Roy. For a while I had that on a customized license plate.

I've done a lot of traveling across the United States and around the world, but I've said many times there is no finer place than the Black Hills of South Dakota. No mosquitoes, no humidity, no sweltering heat: It's just ideal.

But we've also had a lot of fun in our own neighborhood in Sioux Falls.

A Scout is...loyal and cheerful

Chapter 17
FRIENDS AND NEIGHBORS

We began our life in Sioux Falls in a rental house I had found in early January 1958. But that summer, Rodora, the three children and I moved to 2320 Crestwood Road. It was a neighborhood filled with families close in age, and we would have block parties, closing the street off and moving picnic tables out to the middle. Ken Miller was designated as mayor of Crestwood Road.

But after seven years on Crestwood Road, we wanted a larger house and we moved to 1515 E. 30th Street. To make it easy for people to remember, I tell them, "15 plus 15 equals 30th Street." That's the address we use, but the house actually faces Wayland Court. We actually only moved a block away, so we were able to keep our good neighbors.

We were a close-knit neighborhood, and we did a lot of things together. That included getting together for card parties, celebrating birthdays and anniversaries, and playing pranks on each other. We were always doing something. It was all in fun, and nobody got hurt.

Bob Souter worked full time with his father in the family plastering business and part time for me at the hardware store. Bob took life seriously. You didn't want to pull too many tricks on him. But I remember one that involved his black Labrador dog, which sometimes got out in the neighborhood. I had a friend with the Sioux Falls Police Department, and one day he came to the store, wearing his uniform, and presented Bob with a summons, saying someone had complained about his dog running around the neighborhood. I know involving a police officer in a prank would be a no-no today, but we did that then.

After the police officer left, Bob was upset so he jumped in his car and drove to the office of his wife's cousin, who was an attorney. The cousin opened the summons – and there was an invitation to Bob and Donna to go out to dinner to celebrate their wedding anniversary! Bob never lived that down.

We pulled a classic prank on Lew Menzel, who was a teacher and then an assistant principal with the Sioux Falls School District. The Menzels loved a party. We would play cards until 11:00 at night, then Rodora and I would go to bed, and Lew and Ruby would find another place to play cards for another hour or so.

The Menzels had moved to a new place on 32nd Street, and we knew they wouldn't suspect anything when five couples showed up at their door for an unexpected housewarming party. But first, we drove to a farm near Harrisburg owned by Russ Davis's father-in-law and collected fresh cow pies. Ruby was up at their church, and we told Lew to get her so we could welcome them to their new home. That gave us time to take the cow pies, place them on waxed paper, and scatter them around the house – in the dresser drawers, in the fireplace, out in the garage. The cow pies were everywhere.

Best of all, when we all left that night, we told Lew, "Lew, there's 50 of them." But there really were only 49! I don't know how long it took them to find all those cow pies.

Another prank we pulled on Lew involved borrowing a car jack and using it to move his car in the garage so it was sideways. But that joke ended up being on us, because between the time he got home from school and we arrived to take them out to dinner, he had slowly backed up the car, inches at a time, steering it to its original position. When we peeked in the garage windows everything was back to normal.

Lew pulled a prank on me that involved the U.S. Postal Service. Howard Wood, then the postmaster, was going to a small town on business. Lew gave him a package and paid to have the box mailed back special delivery. At 10:30 p.m. the doorbell rang, and I received a package. The sender was marked I.M. Smart – and the box contained another cow pie disguised as a lemon meringue pie, my favorite kind! John and Mary Wiedmeier had moved to Montana, and my first thought was they had done it. So I called them – collect – to make my accusation. Of course, innocent, they were dumbfounded at my charge!

By the way, their son, Bryan Wiedmeier, a longtime executive with the Miami Dolphins, in January 2010 was named the Cleveland Browns' executive vice president of business operation. You never know where these kids who once played in your yard will end up!

When Ruby Menzel gave birth to their fourth child, a son named Rich, some of us went to the Menzels and hung panties all over his tree. Six years later, when Rodora gave birth to Marin, Lew went to my store, used the letter stencils that we had for our printing, and spray-painted a sign to hang across our house's balcony: "The old squirrel had a girl." A neighbor named Bill Haggar, who worked for the Argus Leader, sees this, and he wrote in the paper, "Boy, Roy Nyberg had a unique way of introducing that he had a newborn daughter: 'The old squirrel had a girl,'" implying that my wife was the old squirrel. After that was printed, I went to the bank, and a teller said to me reproachfully, "Roy, how could you?" So it went among our friends, on and on and on.

Not all of our good times happened in Sioux Falls. I was always happy to take anyone up to Minnesota's Boundary Waters where we could canoe and hike. Our Savior's youth pastor, the Rev. Ray Engh, and I led groups of high school students up there before they started their senior year for several summers, and I also took friends I had made through the National Retail Hardware Association.

On one excursion with the high school students, we told them to make sure that their canoe had two packs inside it every time we departed from shore. The second day, we spent the early morning on a portage about 1½ miles long. When we stopped for lunch, we discovered someone had left the lunch pack behind. That was crucial because the pack had not only that day's lunch but the noon meal for every day on the trip.

A tall, lanky youth named Darwin Gilbertson offered to go back with me. We had to go as fast as possible because when you're on a week-long trip, you have to be at a certain location every night.

Darwin and I stripped our canoe of its packs, took two paddles and turned around to travel the three hours back. I have never been in a canoe that has gone any faster. We developed a rhythm that made it sail. It was really fun. Even at the speed we were traveling, however, we didn't rejoin the group until about 11:00 p.m. We didn't have a flashlight so we had to yell until we got their attention and we could find them.

I remember the trip when our National Retail Hardware Association lobbyist wanted to go along. Shelly London was kind of a burly individual, and, boy, was he going to get in shape for this canoe trip. He worked out at the YMCA, but despite being fit, he soon found out that the outdoors was not his comfort zone. He couldn't keep that canoe going straight. His boy was with him, and his son finally got in the boat's stern because Shelly couldn't keep up with us. In the meantime we went through some portages that are a mile and a quarter long, and "Nyberg," I could hear him hollering in the woods, "Nyberg, you beast, you beast." So with Shelly, I'm "The Beast."

Lew Menzel came to the Boundary Waters with me once. I had my eleven-year-old son, Kevin, along, and Lew brought his son, Rich, who was eight. We wanted to go to Hanson Lake and fish for trout. It was windy, and we draped raincoats over our paddles and sailed quickly eastward. I told Lew not to worry because the wind always goes down at night. But that night, it didn't. And here we were, two adults who needed to deliver two children back to camp over 1½ miles of choppy waves. It was getting dark, the kids were in shorts, and the mosquitoes were biting. Finally, we tied birch limbs to the gunnels of the canoes and paddled back to camp that way.

On the same trip, Kevin and I were canoeing when we came to a portage. We decided to shoot the rapids. Normally you wouldn't do that, but these were only about a block long so we decided to give it a try. But I said I was going to take the stern; I was going to be the guy controlling the canoe.

So we hit the rapids, and we're doing fine until all of a sudden – SMACK! We're stuck! The canoe had settled right into the V of a rock beneath the water. Here we are in the middle of rapids, and we have to get out and get soaked so we can pull the canoe free.

We had some great times on those trips. The only really bad experience that I remember was with my son-in-law, Rick; his brother; my son Kevin; Rick Knobe, the mayor of Sioux Falls; his dad; and Dick Buehler, a friend from Western Bank, and his son. But it wasn't the company that was poor, it was the weather. It rained the whole week! It was just an uncomfortable trip.

On that trip, we came to the home of Dorothy Molter, the "Root Beer Lady." She had moved into the wilderness area at Ely, Minnesota, to take care of her dad and loved it so much she stayed there year-round. She would make root beer and sell it for twenty-five cents a bottle. She had a cabin, but in the summers she would live in a tent. She didn't have a dock, but visitors would pull their boats up to a rock ledge. Knobe said to her, "I've got these old parking meters. If I send one of these out to you, would you put it up on the ledge?" She said yes, and he followed through, buying the meter and sending it to her. It was there for years until Dorothy died and the state removed everything.

Because of my *involvement* with the National Retail Hardware Association board, I had gotten some of my fellow members up to the Boundary Waters. But several others were hunters, and because they knew I was from South Dakota, they asked, "Oh, man, do you have any place to hunt? We'd like to come hunt pheasants." Kevin knew a girl from Augustana College who lived near Presho. Her dad owned 3,000 acres, and we started hunting there. Later on, there was going to be a charge of $50 a day per hunter. So we decided to look for our own hunting place. Auctioneer Les Miller found 700 acres near White Lake for us, then 300 more acres came up for sale, so we have 1,000 acres for hunting.

At first we would rent rooms in a White Lake motel. After a couple years, Kevin was preparing to build a store on Sycamore Avenue, and he purchased several houses on his selected property. A friend said to me, "Roy, what are you going to do with those buildings? I'd like to take one of those down to my place for hunting." A light bulb came on! We moved one of those houses 115 miles and developed what I call "The Shack." It's got five bedrooms, with four bunks in each, four showers, dishwashers and microwaves and carpets. It's really not a shack. But it's a great way to bring people out to South Dakota and *expose* them to this *environment* and what the state has to offer.

I love being outdoors. For so many years, I was *involved* with various committees, boards, agencies and activities that it sometimes was hard to get outdoors. But I always made time for doing what I love to do.

A Scout is...friendly and cheerful

Chapter 18
POLITICS AND OTHER ACTIVITIES

Despite all the activities I took part in, sometimes I would say no when asked to join a board or an organization. When I did, it was because I just knew I didn't have enough time to do a good job, and sometimes I knew there were people who could do a better job. Too often, people are asked to join boards because of their money or influence. I think some of these boards would be better served just by having more regular people becoming *involved*.

I also did not become as *involved* in politics as I might have wanted to. People are quick to quit patronizing a business if the owner's politics don't mesh with theirs. It's unfortunate, but it happens.

I speak from first-hand knowledge because one year I publicly supported Tom Daschle, a Democrat who had served four terms in the U.S. House of Representatives. He was running for U.S. Senate against a Republican incumbent, Jim Abdnor. I was active in Republican politics. I even was precinct chairman for a while. I lean toward the Republican Party because I am conservative. But sometimes in this town it's almost a law that if you're a businessman, you must belong to the GOP. To me, it's the candidate that matters more than the party. I have said many times to many people, I bet I have voted more for a Democratic candidate than most Democrats have voted for Republican candidates. I suppose you would call me an independent then.

When Daschle came along, I thought he was a good man who could do a lot for South Dakota. I remember going to a rally at the fairgrounds and speaking out for him. It was easy for me to do at the time, but if I had to do it all over again I wouldn't because I was a businessman, and it drew Republican wrath down on my head. People sent me letters saying, "Roy, how could you?" One came from Marvis Hogen, a good friend, who had followed me on the Minnesota-Dakotas Hardware Board. He was a hardware store owner from Kadoka and served as a Republican in the South Dakota Legislature.

Morris Murphy, president of the Sioux Falls Chamber of Commerce, once thought I'd done a good job as one of his committee chairmen. He was a strong supporter of Abdnor, and now all of a sudden I had lost his favor.

But I felt then and still think today that Daschle was good for the state. When you're in Daschle's presence, you feel like a good friend. I became close to him, and he asked Marin to be the Cherry Blossom Princess in Washington, D.C., when she was a junior in high school. Daschle has visited Rodora and me at our cabin. As a senator, he called several times and asked me to come to the airport while he was waiting for a flight so he could ask me questions. One time he just came right out and said, "You know, I love talking to you because you always screw my head on straight."

I also have been involved in Sioux Falls politics. In 1971, a radio announcer named Rick Knobe began broadcasting on KCHF, a radio station owned by Red Stangland. His radio name was Rick Jeffries. Knobe showed up at my office one day in early 1974. I would record my own radio ads, and Knobe stopped by to pick up the tapes. He was wearing a suit, and he said to me, "Roy, what do you think if I was to run for mayor?" The current mayor, M.E. "Mike" Schirmer, had served since 1968. This was January or February, and the election was in April.

And I gulped and said, "You don't mind losing, do you?" But then I looked at Knobe and said, "All right, I'll tell you what, we'll go down to Here's Johnny's and talk." We went to the restaurant on West 41st Street and sat at the front window. And I gave him this advice. The one thing that politicians do, I said, was go for the big bucks. They always want the big money. "What you want to do, Rick, is try to get as many one dollars as you can from as many people as you possibly can," I said. "Because if you get a buck from them they're going to vote for you." They're basically paying for the privilege of voting for a candidate. It's a combination of *exposure* and *involvement*.

Drawing on my expertise as a problem-solver, I listed three or four things that I felt Knobe had to do to win that election. And I promised my support. I was not a big fan of Schirmer for several reasons, and there was something about Knobe I liked. About half a dozen of us became his promoters, and I was his biggest contributor with a $75 donation. With five candidates in the primary, Schirmer placed first but didn't have the 50 percent plus one vote to win. Knobe finished in second place, about 400 votes back. The third-place finisher was only TWO votes behind him. Two weeks later, Knobe won the run-off election and began what he calls on KSOO radio's Web site "the period in the city's history commonly known as the 'Good Years.' " He says today he wouldn't have won without my support and that I was one of only a very few business people to stand behind him.

A third experience with politics came when about five of us – Jerry Noonan, a CPA; Augustana professor Tom Magstad; veterinarian Tom Ludgate; Duane Burman, a business consultant; and I – created the organization TIGER, which was in existence for about three years. Journalist Maxine Krough helped as our adviser. TIGER stood for Taxpayers for Improved Government Efficiencies and Responsiveness. If there's ever a lesson of politics, that's the one. Because as an individual there's no purpose in going out and trying to change the world. But the total membership of TIGER was five guys, yet we had the newspaper and radio stations calling us up, "Now what would your organization do if thus and thus occurred?" We even had a city commissioner coming to us and wanting our blessing on certain projects. When it comes to politics, you don't know where the arrow could be shot from. And just the five of us, crazy!

I spent just a fraction of my time on politics. There also were church activities. In the late 1990s Rodora and I had left Our Savior's Lutheran Church and eventually found a new church home at Peace Lutheran. I've continued my earlier church involvement there.

I served on the board for Lake Shetek, a Lutheran camp near Slayton, Minnesota.

I was chairman of the Augustana College Business Advisory Council and served on the Sioux Falls Chamber of Commerce board, the South Dakota Unemployment Insurance Advisory Council, the Boy Scouts' Sioux Council board, a Federal Reserve subcommittee, the Sioux Falls Credit Bureau, which then was headed by Milt Husby ... the list goes on and on. Kevin said to me one day, "Dad, how'd you have time for all this?" and I'm beginning to wonder myself!

The reasons I joined some groups varied. For example, I became a member of the Safety Council after I was hit by a car south of the downtown YMCA. The city was going to widen Minnesota Avenue, and as a businessman on that street, I had to be concerned about that. So I was part of the Minnesota Avenue Study.

For a couple years in the 1970s, Rodora and I were members of the Metropolitan Dinner Club of Greater Sioux Falls, which had as its motto this quote by Pulitzer Prize-winning historian Will Durant: "Good food, good company, good minds!" Gerald and Betty Davis served as club patriarchs. The club was limited to 500 people with a membership fee of $20 per couple, $10 for an individual. The men would put on tuxedos and the women formal gowns, and we'd go out for a meal and to hear a nationally known speaker.

As president, Rodora and I would host the speakers in our home. Carleton Smith of Lichtenstein wrote in our guest book in 1973, "A home is a great joy to visit." In 1974 visiting speaker Roger Conklin of Key Biscayne, Florida, wrote, "The warmth of your welcome makes the cold outside evaporate in the sun you create."

For 1974-1975, our list of possible speakers included U.S. Senator Barry Goldwater, CBS newsman Charles Kuralt and political columnist Jack Anderson. The club continued about three years before speakers became too expensive.

When I first moved to Sioux Falls I focused on the hardware store, but I did join the South Sioux Kiwanis Club right away. I had ten years of perfect attendance, but then it was 1969 and I was building the store and my father was diagnosed with cancer. Kiwanis stresses perfect attendance, and I knew I couldn't do it. I quit Kiwanis and joined the Morning Optimists. My kids remember my membership in that club fondly because the Morning Optimists would host a big Thanksgiving breakfast at the Holiday Inn in downtown Sioux Falls, and oatmeal with ice cream on it would be served.

My family has belonged to the Masons for years. My Uncle John's wife gave me the Masonic ring that my grandfather wore. It's over 100 years old. My grandmother was a Worthy Matron in the Order of Eastern Star, as was my mother. For a long time my Uncle John, Mother's brother, did not become a Mason, and I thought it was important to carry on the family tradition. Koochiching Lodge in International Falls was my home lodge, but I received my first three degrees at the Ark Lodge in Minneapolis.

I received the next 14 degrees in Hibbing, then moved to Sioux Falls. I joined the Masonic lodge here, but I didn't become involved right away. A lot of people don't understand what the Masons do and think it replaces church in a person's life. That's not true. It is a fraternal and charitable group that basically asks its members to live a righteous life. After I reached the 32nd degree of Masons, I joined the Scottish Rite, then the Shrine. That was in the late 1970s.

Right away I became a clown with the Shriners, taking the name LeDuke. As a clown I used to watch for teenage girls, sitting on the curb with glum faces, not really happy at being at a parade. I would holler out, "Smile if you're cute.!" Then, after I got a smile, I would say, "Now don't lose it!'

I continued with clowning until 1997 when I took honorary status. The Shriners do a lot of good work. I'm proud of the Shrine hospitals across the country. To this day, whenever possible I serve as a driver, taking children up for treatment at the Shriners Hospital in Minneapolis. People don't realize that if they have a child with orthopedic problems, a Shriners hospital will treat their child at no cost.

We call the children we help Shriner babies because usually we get those children when they're just infants. But once a Shriner baby you're always a Shriner baby. I was talking recently with a woman at Peace Lutheran and I said something about driving a child to the

Shriners Hospital, and she said, "I'm a Shriner baby." And she was close to my age.

I have coffee regularly with a man named John Vanderwaal. His wife's brother is eighty-some years old, and when he was in grade school, he spent three or four months at the Shriners Hospital in Minneapolis. We were traveling to buy novelties for the Shrine circus one day, and we stopped in Elk Point. A young girl who was waiting on us had a bit of a limp. We said something about the Shrine hospitals, and she said, "I know. I'm a Shriner baby," and she slapped her prosthesis. So you never know who you've helped.

By the way, that coffee group has met for 52 years, although we have dropped down from every weekday to three times a week. But at 9:00 a.m. I go to a location that has varied over the years, and we spend an hour solving all the world's problems. We once had as many as 12 people who might show up. It's down to four now, but I value those years of friendship.

In addition to the decades I've spent being part of the Masons, I also have spent almost 50 years with the Elks and first joined the Veterans of Foreign Wars in 1948. While my memberships in those three groups are long-term, I never was as active as some others. I never tried to be. I knew I just didn't have the time to devote to a Masonic Lodge, an Elks club or the VFW.

I also limited some of my after-hours activities with various clubs and organizations. I call the people who always head to a bar after such gatherings "after-glow extremists." Good or bad, I was a loner at such times. Maybe it goes back to my dad's admonition about knowing when to stop drinking.

I found something satisfying in all the agencies, clubs and committees I was part of, although when I retired I walked away from many of them. I needed a break.

But the group I'm proudest of was an organization of volunteers known as RISE. It eventually changed the way Sioux Falls looks today.

A Scout is...trustworthy and brave

Chapter 19

THE BIG SIOUX RIVER

The outdoors – being in the outdoors and encouraging others to be *exposed* to nature – always has been one of my passions. From boyhood, growing up in an area scarcely removed from being a wilderness, I have loved being outside.

That didn't change when my family and I moved to Sioux Falls, a community founded on the prairie around its namesake falls. The Big Sioux River winds through the city, offering recreational opportunities that for many years went unheralded.

The river itself, a tributary of the Missouri River, rises in Roberts County, north of Watertown and more than two hours away from Sioux Falls. In Sioux Falls, it tumbles over a waterfall, and as the river flows south it defines the state line between South Dakota and Iowa. Eventually it joins the Missouri River at Sioux City, Iowa.

In the early 1960s, as part of my community *involvement*, I agreed to serve on the Chamber of Commerce's City Beautification Committee. Members included Mayor V.L. Cruisenberry; Art Hoehl, from the Sioux Falls School District; Hazel O'Connor, a Sioux Falls woman who had a deep love for this city; and Earl McCart, then city parks commissioner.

Earl and I had a relationship that went back several years. I would urge him to create sliding hills where toboggans could be used. I had enjoyed the sport for years and wanted to see others *exposed* to the thrill of winter aboard a toboggan. That is how the hill at Tuthill Park became a snow slide. Unfortunately, toboggans are forbidden now, and slides where the sport can be enjoyed no longer exist.

During a committee meeting, several members who had grown up in Sioux Falls started reminiscing about their youthful activities on the Big Sioux River. They said they would climb on a tire swing and soar over the river before letting go and splashing in the water.

I couldn't believe it. I had been on the river, and there wasn't much water there anymore. Lew Menzel and I, with our children alongside, would walk the frozen river in the winter, Sunday after Sunday after Sunday. In the summer we climbed in canoes and paddled in what little water there was. The first time Lew and I canoed down the river, I said, "It doesn't even seem like we're in Sioux Falls, it seems like we're up in northern Minnesota, in the woods." In the summer, that area was absolutely gorgeous.

But I knew, as did several others, that it could be so much more. That's how a discussion about improving the river emerged from the City Beautification Committee and the vision of a twenty-mile greenway around the Sioux River came into being.

Little of the river bank was under city control. Either it was privately owned, or it was managed by the U.S. Corps of Engineers. Changing that was an early goal.

But first we needed to come up with a structure, and Operation RISE, the River Improvement Study and Evaluation, was born. It was a separate entity from the City Beautification Committee. I became its first chairman. By March 1968 I was speaking at a conference on "Urban Renewal in Rapid City and Sioux Falls." The title of my speech: "How One Man Accepted a Challenge."

We dreamed big from the beginning. An early story in the Argus Leader, dated August 11, 1967, quotes me as saying the "basic idea of the plan is to make the river attractive." That eventually included proposals for such things as:

- A scenic park on both sides of the Big Sioux River from 10th Street to Cherry Rock Bridge;
- An open-air theater below Tuthill Park;

- Highway rest areas just north of 26th Street and west of Interstate 229;
- A marina for water activities south of the YMCA's Leif Ericson Day Camp, which had just had land donated for it in 1966;
- A science park at Tuthill Park near Cliff Avenue with a national science and conservation museum and botanical garden;
- A park representing Oriental culture and landscape, a short distance downstream from the science park, which featured several pagodas. There also was to be a "Garden of Love."

One of the first projects we tackled was a way to raise the river level. By September 1967, engineers Dan Spencer and Don Kalda Sr. were surveying the Sioux River looking for the best location for a collapsible dam, suitable for the downtown area, that would raise the water level for beautification and recreation purposes.

We pursued that inflatable dam for a long time, but there were many obstacles in our path. We knew what we wanted – a fabridam built by the Firestone Tire & Rubber Company. Files I have donated to the Center for Western Studies at Augustana College reveal how long and fervently we pursued it. Its advantages were many: It was described as economical, it wouldn't jam or clog, it would allow flood run-off, it provided pool control, it required an acceptable level of maintenance and it was versatile.

Officials from Firestone even came to Sioux Falls from Akron, Ohio. But the right location to place the fabridam could never be agreed upon and the actual cost –at one time we were told we needed three dams – was prohibitive. In November 1968 we were told it would cost $160,540, and we didn't have that kind of money.

Undaunted, we sought others who could see the vision we shared. Early "verbal volunteer" commitments came from A.F. "Slim" Amburn, Bechtold Jewelry, Howard Bates, Steve Everist, Milt and Mary Husby, Bill Kunkel – people from all walks of life in Sioux Falls. One of the volunteers, John Stencil, has this note penciled behind his name: youngster. Gordon Olson, then the chamber's executive director and someone I thought of as "Mr. Sioux Falls," was a strong supporter.

Richard Beck, then the manager of a popular drive-in known as The Barrel, proposed hiring kids to clean up the Big Sioux River. He noted that much "wooden" debris had accumulated in the Falls Park area, while other parts of the riverbank in downtown Sioux Falls were cluttered with paper, cans and small branches.

What eventually arose from that suggestion was not the hiring of youngsters to clean the river but a group of volunteers who were willing to tackle the necessary job. The first Earth Day was April 22, 1970, and we weren't far behind. We had the first of what was for many years an annual clean-up day on May 22, 1971.

By July 2, 1968, I had made my fifteen presentation to a civic group on the advantage of raising the Sioux River water level and improving its recreational activities. I had agreed to be chairman only if I had a co-chairman, and Jack Gerken offered to fill that role. But early the next year, his profession required him to move to the Black Hills, and I found myself the sole chairman after all, as well as planning the new store at 41st Street and Minnesota Avenue.

But a lot of volunteers supported me, and enthusiasm was growing. In the July 5, 1968, Argus Leader an editorial headline proclaimed "Bold River Dream Is Worth The Try."

That fall, a group of us boarded a Learjet and headed to San Antonio, Texas, which had become famous for its River Walk. It was created along the San Antonio River after a disastrous flood in 1921 led residents to begin making plans to control the river. Today it contains a network of walkways along the river banks one story beneath downtown San Antonio.

I told a local newspaper reporter we were spending two days in San Antonio to gain "insight into the problems that San Antonio found and overcame in their River Improvement Program." Northern Natural Gas out of Omaha sponsored the trip. It was looking for communities interested in preserving access to area rivers and sent a couple men along. Also accompanying me were George DeGroot of

Cengas, a natural gas company that received supplies from Northern Natural Gas; Don Kalda Sr., the RISE engineer; park board member Ernie Carlson; Larry Dirksen, a newsman from KSOO; and Jim Iosty, today an attorney but then a student at Washington High School. It was a good visit and left us charged up and eager to make progress in Sioux Falls.

We then were put in touch with George T.C. Peng, a University of Nebraska professor who took up our project, using his students to help create designs for our dream. That riverfront plan from 1969 stands as the first blueprint, an Argus Leader reporter wrote in 2007, for the bike trail corridor that was completed in 2007. As you can tell, *involvement* often requires a lot of patience.

Others helped us refine our dream. Milo Norwick, then the Sioux Falls director of recreation, listed what could be done on the river: fishing, skating, curling, shuffleboard, sailing, shows and races in the winter; fishing, swimming, canoeing, water shows, paddle boats, hiking on shore, bike paths, bird-watching and nature study, camping, and jogging in the summer.

In October 1968, Stewart Udall, then Secretary of the Interior, came to a local Chamber of Commerce National Affairs Committee meeting, and he spoke on making the river a community asset.

Also in 1968, Dr. Will Rosine, an Augustana College professor, suggested keeping part of the area in its natural state so it could be used as a field lab. Suggestions such as those have eventually occurred in one form or another. For example, today we have The Outdoor Campus, open since 1997, which offers environmental learning.

In December 1968 we underwent a name change to the Sioux Falls River Improvement Society. But we forever would be known by the initials RISE.

Officers of the Sioux Falls River Improvement Society included Jack Gerken, my friend Lew Menzel, assistant principal at Washington High School, and Hazel O'Connor. Her greatest interest was in restoring Falls Park to its past glory, mine was to improve the Sioux River, but our dreams meshed together perfectly. I admired her greatly.

Other early board members include Edmund Beck, city planning director; R.E. Bragstad, city engineer emeritus; Ray Jorgenson, city engineer; Ernie Carlson, George DeGroot, Larry Dirksen, Russel Eng, the Rev. Ray Engh from Our Savior's Lutheran, James Iosty, Donald Kalda, Mrs. Frank Kelly, Darrell Modica, Ken Munro, Leona Nordstrom, Ed Pierce, Richard Sayre, and Dan Spencer. And we had so many other supporters who played essential roles, people like Marlo Schultz, Stanley Morrill and Dr. G.I.W. Cottam. The more I list, the more I fear I will forget others.

In November 1969, we conducted a membership drive to raise money. We stated our goals this way:

- Clean and improve the river banks for scenic and useful development;
- Raise water level for boats and winter sports;
- Develop various but integrated recreational, educational and scenic facilities; and
- Attract new and better residential development.

We had taken out a loan in September 1969, borrowing $1,471 from a local bank. It was due March 1, 1970. Lew Menzel, Hazel O'Connor and I signed for the loan.

We were dreaming big. Peng's plan, in particular, had several proposals that sounded good on paper but weren't likely to come to pass. Dr. Cottam noted in one correspondence, "The Sioux Tower may need to be a very tall Tepee, modified." It was to include a restaurant.

Even supporters sometimes kept their hands firmly in their pockets when it came to finances. Some early campaigns for funds produced bleak results. "To get the needed money by solicitation seems hopeless," one record notes. "We were only able to get a few hundred in our bank account."

Plus, not everyone supported us. Two realtors and an oil company opposed our proposed rezoning of the riverbank. We wanted it to be zoned recreational; they wanted it for commercial uses. Without rezoning, we knew we could not proceed. There was another obstacle always in our way: the cost of things. An article quotes the committee as saying, "If we get it zoned, all we need is MONEY." Dues in 1970 were $2.50 per member; such a pittance didn't raise a lot of funds.

In 1970, we went before city boards to oppose the development of riverbank property at 26th Street and Interstate 229 by Continental Oil Company, also known as Conoco. The property was zoned single-family housing; Conoco sought a change to commercial, while RISE wanted it to be conservation. The Planning Commission approved the change 2-1; only Parks Commissioner McCart sided with us. In the end, Conoco gave us the land because the company didn't want the controversy. We asked the state to make the northeast corner of that intersection a rest stop, and eventually we got a park there.

In the meantime, people began looking for ways to use the river. The Jaycees conducted river regattas for several years, the first one in May 1971, and it became a source of more recreational activities.

We had accomplished a lot, but we had further to go. In March 1970, I stepped down as president, with Marlo Schultz replacing me, but remained on the board. I left the board in August 1973, saying it was extremely difficult to keep enthused when I found myself on the defensive because of my support for RISE. I had been the lightning rod for too many years for those who didn't see what a great thing this could be.

This kind of thing can't be a one-man project, you know, but even after I stepped back I always followed RISE's progress. In 1992 I was back on the board and served as vice-president in 1995. Earlier, in 1991, I was named to the Phillips to the Falls Task Force and helped realize my old friend Hazel O'Connor's dream of making Falls Park a beautiful place once again. She had died in the mid-1980s.

RISE had many successes. The Norlin family donated land so Norlin Parkway could be opened in 1974. RISE banded together to oppose a high-rise apartment in an unsuitable location along the river.

In 1974, Rick Knobe, the man I had supported in his run for mayor, took office. One of his first acts as mayor was to ask the City Planning Commission to create a plan for the river. The city commissioners adopted the first greenway plan in April 1975. By 1984 the city owned 1,200 acres along the riverbanks.

The entity that was RISE eventually faded away as volunteers grew older, wearier or moved away. It can be discouraging to pursue a dream over decades. In 1997 the minutes show a motion was made to dissolve RISE because of lack of cooperation from the Park Board. Instead, it was decided to study the matter for 30 days. It officially dissolved in May 2002.

But the beauty of the Big Sioux River lives on. And I still have ideas that will make it a place that can be enjoyed by everyone. In June 2007, when the city celebrated the bike trail's completion, I suggested that it would be nice for senior citizens to be able to ride golf carts on the bike trails.

In spring 2009, that came to pass, and I was able to enjoy the river once again, this time not from a canoe but from a motorized golf cart. It was as beautiful as it always had been.

The vision I have for the river that runs through Sioux Falls can be expanded to recreational activities throughout the city. Bike trails, improved canoeing, more soccer fields – we have done so much, but we have so much more to offer.

On my honor I will do my best

Chapter 20
RETIREMENT AND TRAVEL

As a businessman, I know how important it is to treat people fairly.

I also follow this practice in my personal life. An example is the time I decided to trade in my SUV. I went to a local car dealership and made arrangements to buy a new vehicle. When I was asked if the old car had been in an accident, I said, yes, but I remembered the damage as less than $5,000.

However, when I looked up the repair bill at home I discovered my memory was faulty. It had cost $7,000 to repair the Tahoe. When I went back the next day to sign the papers, I reported my error. The used-car manager called the deal off.

I ended up going to another dealership, which made me a better offer. I bought the car there, but I called my original salesman and asked him to come to my house. There I gave him a personal check for $200 to make up for his commission he lost due to my error. It wasn't his fault that the sale fell through, and I didn't think it was right he should suffer financially.

As Kevin did on that snowy Christmas Day for the couple who needed a sewer snake, I often opened up the store when a person needed help. I did it on a holiday for someone who didn't have a fishing license; without one his excursion would be ruined. I also did it when people would blow a fuse and find they didn't have a spare to replace it. In the days before circuit breakers became common, that wasn't an unusual problem. It would only be a sale of five cents or a dime, but I would go down to the store and help them out. You didn't want to leave someone sitting in the dark.

If you have a good attitude, you can enjoy almost anything you do. I've always told my children and my employees that if a job seems to be repetitious, try to figure out a way you can do your work faster but just as efficiently. Ask yourself, is there an easier way to do it? I have the ability to do a job quickly without losing any efficiency, and that has helped me in everything I've done.

I enjoyed my career in business and being a small-businessman immensely. But as I neared my 62nd birthday, I began making plans to step down.

I could retire as early as I did largely because one of my children was interested in taking over the family hardware store. It could have been any one of the four, but as it turned out, it was Kevin who decided that was what he wanted to do for his career.

Kevin returned to the hardware store in 1981 to begin learning the business. In 1983 he suggested that we remove the Native American motif that had decorated the store since its opening in 1969. It looked dated, plus times and attitudes had changed. I didn't object at all.

I thought remodeling was a good idea. Because of the additions, the store's interior had changed drastically, and we had lost the unity it once had. We created uniformity in the store by having one person create all the signs, rather than the old way of letting each department head do it.

We also concentrated on changing people's attitudes toward hardware stores. I had been on a canoe trip with friends once when one of them asked me why people viewed hardware stores as expensive. We all shared our thoughts on that, but I think the one who got it right was an engineer who said, "I think the reason why hardware stores are perceived to be expensive is that they don't show a store that looks 'saley' when people come in." He said it was vital that customers enter a store that is clean, looks like a place where something is happening, is well signed and has good prices on the interior loop that customers walk.

I had started looking at someone succeeding me in business – family or otherwise – in 1977 when I joined the National Retail Hardware Association board. That's when I pushed to have the book "Who's Next Please?" written to help others like me who needed to make adequate plans for the future. I think any store owner who reaches his 55th birthday should have a plan in place.

After Kevin decided he wanted to be the second generation to run Nyberg's Ace Hardware, Rodora and I made sure in our estate planning that we were fair to all four of our children. Rodora and I gave Kevin separate gifts in stock annually. When the total gift reached the allowable amount, Kevin bought the remaining stock. To give our three daughters a fair share, I have purchased a life insurance policy that will be split between them when I die.

Kevin buying the store from us gave us a steady income that permitted us to lead a comfortable life with frequent traveling. He says today he is proud that he has helped us to have a retirement without any worries about money. If Kevin hadn't joined the store, I probably would have worked longer. I would have HAD to work longer. If I'd found a buyer for the store, I could have sold the property or kept it. I don't know which I would have done, but it isn't something I'll have to worry about.

Seven years after Kevin's decision to be a part of the hardware store, I retired in 1988 when I was 62. Because of complications with Social Security, I had to return some early payments, and I didn't fully retire until age 64.

Several times over the years, Kevin has told different publications that he regrets we didn't work together longer. In the May 1988 profile of me in Hardware Merchandiser magazine, "A Voice for the Little Guy," Kevin said, "I don't want him to ever just retire and not have any involvement. I always want him to be there for advice and counseling."

In 2010, in an article in the Sioux Falls Business Journal after we were named the South Dakota Retail Association's Retailers of the Year, Kevin said, "I don't think many sons will say they wished their father wouldn't have retired so early." Reading that brought tears to my eyes. My family TOLD you I was sentimental!

I probably would not have retired as early as I did if Kevin had not been there, ready to take over the store. But I was 32 when I became owner of a hardware store, and Kevin was going to be 32 later in 1988. "He's going to have the same vinegar that I had," I told Hardware Merchandiser magazine. "And if I were to suppress that, he wouldn't blossom out to be the person he's capable of being, just because the old man's hanging around and telling him what to do."

Whenever Kevin asked for help, I was there. But during our retirement, I stepped back from many of my activities, and Rodora and I began traveling around the world, not forgetting places in the United States we wanted to see again. Here's a sampling: 1996, New England and a cruise from St. Petersburg to Moscow; 1997, China; 1998, Norway, Sweden, Finland; 1999, Israel and the Passion Play in Oberammergau; and 2001, Alaska.

I had done a fair amount of traveling before retirement. In addition to the family vacations to convention sites, one year I won a trip from the Weber kettle grill corporation. Rodora and I, along with four others, flew on a Learjet to St. Lucia in the Caribbean. We stayed on a steel-hulled yacht that once was used for drug-running.

Another time, the president and the national sales manager of Scotts, the lawn-care company, asked Bill Aubuchon and me to fly to a house boat in Key West. Bill ran a chain of hardware stores in New England that his family had started in 1908. The purpose of the trip was to give the president and national sales manager one-on-one time with two successful retailers and find out what advice we had for them.

But after retirement, I focused on family trips. One year, realizing that Nancy was the only one of our children not to see Sweden and Norway, we took her with us for three weeks. I have told Nancy that I think about that trip often because we had such a neat time. It also was an opportunity to see Jan Wedsberg, the exchange student from Sweden who stayed with us when Kevin was in high school. We have stayed in touch all these years.

Rodora and I always enjoyed being *exposed* to other lands and cultures, although sometimes we saw things that made us appreciate our own country so much more than we had. I remember going down the Volga River and approaching a town in Russia on a bright sunny day. But the town was smothered in a cloud of smoke and ash. Some of the small towns we visited, it was just like going back in time to South Dakota hamlets in the 1800s. No sidewalks, no paved roads.

In China we saw barren hilltop after hilltop after hilltop, each one stripped of trees. Outside each hut would be a small pile of kindling. Any stick they found, no matter how small, was gathered for future use. We went to an open-air market in China where I saw a chair sitting out in the open. It looked like a barber chair at first glance. But it actually belonged to a dentist. False teeth sat on a nearby table.

We saw temples made of gold, but the people were starving. We saw women who, if they were born on Wednesday, grew up having their necks stretched by adding ring after ring and forcing them to grow. They told us they never wanted that done to their own daughters.

All the traveling we've done, I think that is one of the reasons I get a little bit upset with the demands of people in the United States. Most people do not know how fortunate we are to be living where we are, to be honest. But when you see people who are just like you but living in the worst poverty imaginable, you can never be the same.

Rodora's favorite trip was seeing polar bears. Perhaps that's because it was her idea. One day I said to her, "Oh, that's all you talk about is those darn polar bears. If you want to go so bad, go arrange it." Well, she got up from her chair, went to the phone and called a travel agent and made plans for us to join a tour. We drove to Winnipeg, Canada, then flew to Churchill in Manitoba, right on Hudson Bay, which is nicknamed "the Polar Bear Capital of the World." We rode on tundra buses, vehicles on high wheels, and with only 30 of us, everyone had a window. Rodora says she would recommend that trip to anybody.

The one trip she wouldn't suggest is to the South Sea islands. We went there with good friends, George and Florence Fujiwara. They are Japanese-Americans who live in Hawaii. When George was a boy, he saw the attack on Pearl Harbor, but he thought it was a training exercise. Florence's family had it rough during World War II. They lived in Washington state and were forced to leave their home for an internment camp.

So the company was good and I caught a "grand slam," which in the Marshall Islands is catching a mahi-mahi, ono, ahi and marlin, all salt-water fish. But Rodora didn't enjoy much of our stay. To begin with, Rodora is not crazy about water. So that was a long trip over the ocean. She didn't mind visiting Guam, but our stay on Ponape Island was agony for her. Our hut had a waterbed, which she didn't appreciate. As Rodora says, "If I don't like water, I sure don't like a waterbed." Plus, there were little lizards running around. I was snorkeling in the ocean, and Rodora decided to sit in a grass hut to read. She had barely gotten started with her book when a lizard came crawling up her arm. She gave it one firm swat, and the lizard went sailing. And that was the end of that.

We still get together as often as we can as a family. When you have a happy family, as we do, those get-togethers are always the best times ever.

A Scout is...trustworthy and loyal

Chapter 21
THE KIDS TAKE A TURN

My brother Bob always says the two of us are exact opposites. He describes me as Type A, and he says he's Type B. He worked at Honeywell for 38 years, moving his way up the ranks to management. So he has drive. But he says I'm more outgoing, more of a go-getter. He's quieter and goes about his own business.

We see each other a couple times a year. That's not as often as we'd like, but our own families keep us busy.

As it has been since the beginning, family is important to me. Rodora and I are extremely proud of our nine grandchildren and consider ourselves fortunate that they grew up in Sioux Falls so we could see them often. They are nine good kids.

It is a family joke that on each grandchild's 13th birthday I take them out for a birds-and-the-bees talk. That's not exactly the case. It isn't precisely on their 13th birthday, but it's as close to it as I can make it.

And we don't talk about the facts of life, not in the sense that most people understand it. But I do talk to them about how important *environment*, *exposure* and *involvement* is in their lives, as teenagers and as adults.

As I look back on my own life, I have discovered that every activity in which I participated opened doors for me. I made countless friends through my *involvement*, and often being a member of one organization developed contacts that led to even greater *exposure* elsewhere.

I have taken part in projects that have changed Sioux Falls and been elected to important national office, but I don't think, and I don't mean to sound egotistical, that I ever became self-important. In other words, as I have said many times, I'm not a hot-dogger. I've never thought I was better than anyone else.

Too often in today's world, people do things only because it will benefit themselves. I don't know that I've ever done anything that I purposely wanted it to be of benefit for me. Now having said that, I have had a good life. Things have happened to me that are extraordinary. But I didn't go out of my way to try to be there. I still go back to my days as a Boy Scout. I still think that being trustworthy, loyal, helpful, friendly, courteous, kind, obedient, cheerful, thrifty, brave, clean and reverent is the perfect way to live one's life.

I've shared a lot in the preceding chapters. That's why I thought it was only fair I give my children a chance to speak out, too.

Jody —

It was in the early 1970s that Dad really started focusing on *environment*, *exposure* and *involvement* as the way to lead one's life. I confess, as kids when he would bring it up we'd just roll our eyes and say "Here he goes again." It was 1972 or '73 that he had the sign with those three words on it made for his office.

I was involved in school but not to the extent that kids are today. I was captain of the Patriettes, the Lincoln High School drill team, played in the orchestra, and participated in other school activities. One thing I do regret is that I stopped playing when I went to college. I thought it was not cool to play violin when I was in college. I was a Job's Daughter, because Dad was a Mason. I was in Brownies and Girl Scouts but quit in junior high school when everyone else did. I really did spend a lot of time studying because I wanted to get straight A's.

Dad really pushed us, me in particular, because I was the oldest. And the oldest always has to kind of forge the way for the others. I had kind of a sassy mouth, and I didn't like being told what to do. Dad wasn't an easy guy to work for; he was very demanding. I would say, "Why are you so hard on me?" He'd reply, "I know you are capable of doing more and you can do better."

I was not wild by any means, but I was independent. I grew up in the 1960s, during the Vietnam era. The time of flower power, freedom, hippies and miniskirts. I never did drugs or alcohol for three reasons. First, I didn't want to; second, I ran around with a very good group of friends; but most importantly I had the fear that if Dad found out I'd be grounded for life. I was involved in school. Even now, I'm a leader. When I get involved in something, I get very involved in it. I'm like Dad that way. He used to joke, "It's hard to be humble when you're as great as I am."

Dad was not around that much. Sometimes he would take me to school, but I usually walked because he would be gone before we ever got up in the morning. Gone by seven, home at six, then he'd go back to the store. Especially in the month of December, we'd never see him. Mom, like mothers of the day, did the cooking and made sure we had our chores done. Mom never complained – never. She was really easy-going.

My Nyberg grandparents were very nice and loving. Grandpa was kind of a comical guy. He smoked, so he used to blow smoke in our faces. We thought that was so funny. Today you'd think "second-hand smoke!," but then we thought that was so cool. Grandpa was a jokester and happy-go-lucky. Grandma was really serious, but she was a really nice grandma. She and I spent three weeks touring Europe. Dad said she once had a nervous breakdown, but nobody really talked about it.

Vacations at Rainy Lake were fun, except for the outhouse. And the mosquitoes. The lake was gorgeous, and Grandpa would peel potatoes so Grandma could make a potato pancake breakfast on Sunday mornings. I thought it was so cool to brush your teeth in the lake and take a bath there. The leeches were awful. We always kept a salt shaker on the dock in case we got a leech. You'd sprinkle the salt on them, but we never did get one. Nancy and Kevin would catch frogs and chase me with them because I hated frogs.

While still in junior high, I was in charge of updating the catalogs at the hardware store. Every department had a catalog, and each week, Ace would send new pages with revised pricing and updated pictures. I would take the old pages out of the catalog and put in the new. I made twenty-five or thirty-five cents an hour at the store. When I was older, it was a big deal when I broke a dollar an hour. I remember getting the checks from Ace Hardware. I got paid to work, I was an official employee. We never called him Dad at the store. It was Roy. We didn't want the customers to know we were the owner's kids.

In high school I became a cashier, and when I left college, I was in charge of the other cashiers. We would know almost all the customers and all the construction guys coming in for supplies by name and knew who they worked for. When they came up to the counter, we'd have their charge cards pulled already.

Being *exposed* to the hardware business and knowing people in hardware got me my first job at Warner Hardware, then my job at Farwell Ozmun and Kirk wholesale company. Those people knew how hard I worked and my work ethic. It was a nice progression, from Warner to FOK to Farberware. I left Dad's hardware store because I needed to move on. I never looked back. I grew up there, I learned a lot, but I wanted to move on. I've never regretted not staying.

Nancy —

My dad instilled a respect for others into us kids. In particular, he wanted us to respect our elders, and I think to this day we treat those older than we are with a heartfelt dignity. He also taught us to be kind to everyone, so there isn't a day that goes by that I don't say thank you. Dad helped us realize the importance of thanking someone even for doing the smallest things.

We did fun things as a family. Sunday night we would play table games. One Sunday I might pick out the game Risk, and we'd play that. The next Sunday it would be someone else's turn to select a game.

Every summer there would be a hardware convention somewhere, and we would drive to it. I feel lucky that at 56 years old I have seen every state except for Alaska just from the traveling that we did as a family. The trips to conventions were fun. There were kids from other states whose parents came to the convention, and every year we would meet up with them again.

When my kids were four, six and eight, that's when Dad led the National Retail Hardware Association, so we took them to the convention. It was passed on to the next generation.

Dad always likes to plan the trips. When Dad, Mom and I took the trip to Norway, Sweden and Finland he spoke of earlier, he spent months planning that trip. We rented a car upon our arrival, and we drove through those three countries. It was hard to be gone from my family for three weeks, but I have a husband who is self-sufficient. And this was a once-in-a-lifetime chance. It was a wonderful trip.

Dad and I are like two peas in a pod, really. We are so much alike it's almost scary. One of the things we have in common is we enjoy working with numbers. I did that for 22 years, keeping books at the store.

Dad often comes up with funny things to say. He has a good sense of humor, but I didn't really realize how much until these last few years. He always tells us, "I have a natural smile on my face." So, once in a while if he's complaining about something, I'll tease him by asking, "Where's that natural smile?"

I don't feel like he ever pushed any of us to work at the store when we were in school. He wanted us to focus on our studies and to be *involved* in different activities. I think in high school the only job I had was babysitting, for a quarter an hour. I was in a lot of plays, and I don't think he missed a single one, no matter how busy he was.

Once I had my kids I was able to stay home, thanks to my father. I was able to do the bookwork at home. As they grew older, I would see the kids off to school in the morning and be here when they got home from school. I would set up a big, round table in the living room, and that's where they'd find me after school. When Jennifer went off to kindergarten, that's when I went down to the store to work.

Mom and Dad have always had a strong marriage. I think that's why we four children have such strong marriages, too. I don't remember ever hearing them argue in front of us. If they ever did argue, they did it privately. Rick would do anything for my parents. When he first came home with me, he had his hair in an afro and smoked cigarettes. I sometimes wonder what they thought!

Mom and Dad are so close to their grandchildren. When Rick was 36, he'd already lost both his parents. So Mom and Dad were the only grandparents my kids ever really had. I had fun having two totally different sets of grandparents. Grandpa and Grandma Dokken lived on the farm, and my Grandpa and Grandma Nyberg lived in International Falls and had the cabin on Rainy Lake. So we were *exposed* to two different types of worlds.

One of my contributions to the family comes through a personal diary that I've written in every day since 1969. It's made me something of the family historian, and it's come in handy many times. If any of us needs to know when a special event had occurred, who was there or even what the weather was like, they come to me, and sure enough, I'll have the information. I sometimes joke that these many journals will be buried with me, but I actually hope the collection someday is a gift treasured by my daughters.

Kevin —

There are two words I think describe my dad: visionary and entrepreneurial. Looking at what Dad did with the stores, first the one on South Minnesota Avenue, then the store at 41st Street and Minnesota Avenue, there's no doubt he has vision. Tying in with that is being an entrepreneur. If he had been complacent, content with a 4,000-square-foot store on Minnesota Avenue, there's no doubt he would have been swallowed up by the big box stores that came to town. I don't think Nyberg's Ace Hardware would be around today without those two traits. In some ways, I think visionary and entrepreneurial fit me, too, and my son, Erik. So those traits have been passed down to two generations.

Sometimes I think that perhaps I followed too closely in Dad's footsteps. I expanded the hardware stores: in 1990, at 12th Street and Kiwanis Avenue; in 2000, on East Sycamore Avenue; in 2002, in Brookings, which I've since sold; and in 2004, on Sertoma Avenue. So from 2000 to 2004 it was a crazy, busy time for me. And I was involved in the expansion probably when my four kids needed me the most. I'm proud of the stores, but it took a lot of time and money. Dad went through the same thing when he was expanding his stores.

But you have to ask yourself, would we be the family we are today if Dad hadn't taken risks? Would I have the family I have today if I hadn't taken risks? So there's a trade-off in life, and you have to take risks to be successful.

I don't think Dad regrets not following through on his plans to open a second or third store. What he went through in the late 1960s and early 1970s – the construction workers being electrocuted; losing his father; his partner Ernie Kaiser dying; the death of Harold Slocum, a valued employee; the financial issues – those all had to take a toll on him.

I do wish he had stayed with the hardware store longer. I've not heard of too many sons who say they regret that their dad retired so early. But we could have done some amazing things together because he's the finance guy, I'm the marketing guy.

When I think back, I don't remember my dad ever second-guessing me. I don't really remember him teaching me the business either. But I think now because he did it so generously, so deftly, that I never even realized what he was doing. I learned by observing and listening, I guess. That's how he taught all of us kids and how he shared the principles he lives by: *environment, exposure* and *involvement.*

I probably have a different perspective of my father than my three sisters have because Dad was an outdoors guy, and we spent a lot of time together. My sisters didn't have the same exposure to the outdoors. Again, I guess I could say the same thing about Erik and my three daughters. The girls have their own passions, and Erik and I go pheasant hunting, or we go canoeing, or we go to a Minnesota Twins game, that kind of thing. It was the same with Dad and me.

I sometimes think people have the wrong perception of my dad. They see him as rough, gruff, direct. My hunting buddies were a bit nervous the first time we all went hunting together. They didn't know him well and expected this brusque man. But that's not true at all. There's a compassionate side to Dad that isn't always readily apparent. Maybe he wasn't always as diplomatic as he could have been. But when it came to things like preserving a greenway along the Big Sioux River, he became so passionate about it, he couldn't understand why others didn't feel the same way. Sometimes I think my dad was a bit of a rebel. He never minded challenging others' ideas or the status quo. I don't care if you're talking about city government, the South Dakota Retail Association, the White House Small Business Conference, the Chamber of Commerce – Roy Nyberg was not afraid to speak out.

People sometimes stereotype people in business. They lose sight of the fact that businesspeople have social responsibilities, a strong sense of right and wrong. That's true of my father.

Because of Dad and his involvement, I was able to do a lot of traveling as a boy. I would not have had that kind of exposure – 49 states by the time I was 25 – without that. I have a strong interest in Scandinavian culture and politics because of my father and the *environment* in which he was raised.

Dad is a lucky man when it comes to the woman he married. My mother is an amazing person, reserved but a loving individual. She had to have a lot of patience and tolerance because of him being gone so much to make the store a success and the stress involved in the expansions. We always had supper together when I was a kid, and Dad would pour out his frustrations and his stress to Mom. But Dad will tell you he's had a great life.

When my sisters and I think of my Grandpa Nyberg, we think about going to the lake and picking blueberries. When Dad's nine grandchildren remember him, they'll think of the cabin in the Black Hills and taking part in the Crazy Horse Volksmarch. He has passed on his love of the outdoors to his grandchildren.

One story I enjoy telling about Dad goes back to 1972. I was 16, and my name was drawn to win a black Labrador puppy. Dad and Mom wanted a few days to think about whether I was going to be able to have this dog or not. So Dad turned to a friend of his, accountant Wes Nelson. "Geez, Wes, what do I do, my son won a Labrador?" Wes said, "I'll tell you one thing: If you let that son of yours have that dog, you won't have to worry about him chasing girls for the next four or five years!" Dad saw the wisdom in that. I got the dog, and I really didn't have time to chase girls during high school. I bring that up because it's exposure and environment and involvement. My having that black Lab – and four since then – made such an impact on my life.

Marin —

I always say I'm a lot like my mother, I'm more Norwegian than Swedish. We're the ones who have the low blood pressure in the family. We're not the Type A personalities, we're the ones that sit back and watch. I'm organized like her, too, but I'm sentimental like Dad.

I had a different childhood than Jody, Nancy and Kevin. When it was time to travel to hardware association conventions, instead of three kids crammed into the back seat, it was always just me. We got to see a lot of the countryside and stay at different hotels and eat at different restaurants. We stopped at one restaurant, and all I wanted was grits. Dad ordered his grits, and I said I'd like to have grits, too. The waitress yelled out in this Southern drawl to the cook, "She wants grits just like her daaaaaaaddy." We always bring up the grits story. It was so funny.

With a July birthday that came at convention time, I always had my birthdays in rest stops. We'd pull off to the side of the road, and we'd have a birthday cake with the frosting melting quickly in the heat. But when we got home, I had the normal birthday parties with friends. And I always had the best cakes. One was shaped like a raccoon, because I was into raccoons then, and one shaped like a record, Marie Osmond's "Paper Roses," and one time it was actually shaped like a piano.

Music is something that runs through my childhood. We always had music playing in the house. I would spend hours going through my vinyl records, selecting which songs I wanted to play next, and singing in the mirror.

Dad and I have this history of dancing at the hardware conventions. You're eating dinner at your table, and then the band starts, and you get up and dance when you want to dance. It's big band music, and our song is "In the Mood." We have our certain steps that we do, it's almost jitterbuggy.

When Dad ran the store, he used to do a lot of the writing of radio advertisements, and he recorded them. That's what I do today. I write the spots, and then I record them. I think I inherited the creativity from my dad. The work ethic, too. It's a different situation because Kevin's my boss, but I don't treat him like a brother at work. I worked for a cheerleading supply company after college, then the company folded up. I applied at the store in June of 1989, and I really made it official: I turned in my cover letter and my application. My husband and I did move to Kansas City for three months in 1996, but we felt it just wasn't right for us.

Something I struggled with through elementary school was my close friends had these young mothers, and Mom had me when she was 35 and Dad 40. I remember like it was yesterday, standing on bleachers in elementary school ready to sing in a chorus concert, and my parents came in the door. I waved, and one of the kids went, "Is that your grandparents?" "Noooo, that's my mom and dad." I would say, "I have such old parents," and Dad would say, "Yes, but you keep us young." So I struggled with that, but then I had my own kids later in life.

I started working at the store when I was nine, helping Mom check in freight and putting price tags on them. During high school I did not work because I was so involved in everything, plus I was very studious, plus I had a boyfriend. My fondest memories of high school are performing in the talent shows, and I was passionate about being a cheerleader. So I wasn't forced to work. Dad must have felt being *involved* in school was very important. During the summers I helped with advertising. I reported to the advertising director; she made out my schedule. But I did a lot of radio ads with Dad.

My folks kept us grounded. We lived really an ordinary life. We never had a fancy house, and we never had fancy cars. What was important to them was that we take advantage of the opportunities we had, that we got *involved*.

A Scout is...courteous and kind

FINAL THOUGHTS

From the beginning of this book, I knew I would be undertaking a new task foreign to my past experiences. This process jogged this older person's memory chip beyond the norm. Jill Callison pulled from me *involvements* and *exposures* long forgotten.

More importantly, since reminiscing started in the fall of 2009 and involved many 4:00 a.m. waking moments to jot down notes that otherwise I would forget, I now am more convinced that my *involvements* and *exposures* in my life have truly opened doors and led to adventures one would normally just dream about.

I must reiterate that my Boy Scout background to this day still fuels my actions. Serving on many boards of directors presented frequent insights and paved the way for me to gain foresight for future opportunities. The honor of serving on an international board also gave Rodora and me the opportunity to take trips, many as long as a week, to approximately 20 countries. These *exposures* gave us a variety of humanitarian compassion.

The first and most rewarding accolade goes to that seventeen-year-old girl who had a spitball thrown at her by a World War II veteran. She paid no attention to a second cousin's advice: He had told her to be careful while attending college because of all the wolves returning from the service!

In this book I have given much credit to the women in my life. However, Rodora truly is the backbone. She has that Norwegian don't-rock-the-boat personality, she raised four strong-minded children, and she has acquainted eight granddaughters to Scandinavian customs, Swedish on my side and Norwegian on hers. And she never left her grandson out either.

Rodora has always been *involved* in and *exposed* to our business decisions. Again, she has been the backbone of our family and, to add another metaphor, the steady rudder of our ship. Thank you, Rodora, for just being you.

Also, thanks to Jill Callison for gathering, researching and substantiating many of my claims to events of yesteryear. She was so thorough that to my amazement she even uncovered stories about my family of which I was unaware.

Looking back, I've found I can say this without hesitation: I've had a good life. It came with a few regrets, but that happens to us all. Anyway, Rodora and I are still here and still enjoying our life together.

Roy Duke Nyberg
July 2010

EPILOGUE

Roy Duke Nyberg died at Sanford Hospital in Sioux Falls on September 6, 2010, of pulmonary fibrosis. He had told his kids and grandchildren from his hospital bed, "I'm not done teaching yet." Jill Callison delivered the first draft of this book to him on September 1st. That afternoon, he told me he wanted to "go on that breathing machine," full aware that his decision could be irreversible.

I made the sign of the cross on his forehead and reminded him of words spoken at his baptism: "Roy Duke Nyberg, child of God, you have been sealed by the Holy Spirit and marked with the cross of Christ, forever." He nodded his head vigorously when I finished.

Five days later, he spared his family the decision to take him off life support when, with great effort, he pulled out the breathing tube. Informed of his action, the entire family gathered around his bed with thanks and goodbyes while Pastor Gene Tjarks read Psalm 121 and John 14.

Peace Lutheran Church was filled on September 10th, and we celebrated with bagpipes, Boy Scouts, Scripture, tributes, hymns and prayers. The service was followed by food, including Swedish meatballs. We shared love, humor, faith and playfulness - traits which characterized Roy.

Obed Nelson,
personal friend and pastor

After the service to celebrate Roy's life, his family gathered on the greenway bordering the Big Sioux River, which Roy had done so much to preserve for future generations.

Mary Jane Gentry, born December 8, 1854, was my mother's grandmother. She married John Green Duke, born July 18, 1847, and they lived in Tennessee during the Civil War. Known as "Mammy," she was 84 in this photo. I met her only once. *(Chapter 1)*

Walter Alvin Wirt and Jessie Duke Wirt were my grandparents. They were married in Tennessee on December 3, 1902, and moved to International Falls when my mother was nine. *(Chapter 1)*

Olaf (Eskilsson) Nyberg and Marie (Lindberg) Nyberg were married January 26, 1886, in Sweden. They are my father's parents. Some of my grandfather's brothers changed their last names to Eskilsson and Wikner. *(Chapter 1)*

My father, Nils Otto Nyberg, and my mother, Helen Ruth Wirt, were married on June 23, 1925, at the International Falls Methodist Church. *(Chapter 1)*

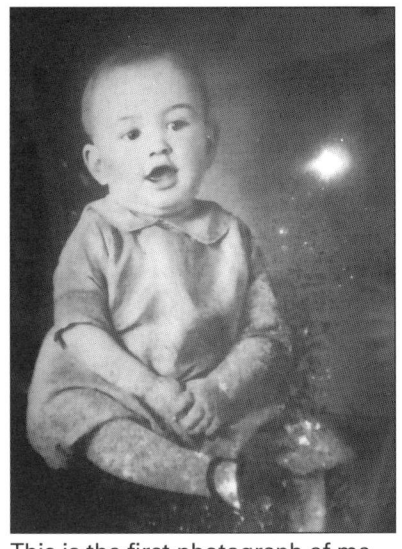

This is the first photograph of me at nine months old. *(Chapter 1)*

My mother's sisters loved playing with my brother, Bob, and me. Jessie Lee "Wewe" is on the left and Florence "Sissy" is on the right. *(Chapter 1)*

Don Enzman (bottom), his brother Art "Skeezix" and my brother, Bob, show how we had to bundle up to play outside. Bob and I often played with the Enzman boys. Their mom was like our second mother. *(Chapter 2)*

I'm about 5½ and Bob is 18 months in this photo. Notice the bib overalls I'm wearing; it was a typical boy's outfit for the time. *(Chapter 2)*

This is me preparing for my paper route. I started selling papers at the age of six. *(Chapter 2)*

I am sitting in the stern of a Scout canoe in the summer of 1942. Black Bay is in the background. *(Chapter 3)*

I took this photograph of the Ace Hardware in International Falls several years ago. According to the Ace Hardware numbering system, it was Store No. 66. Now stores are numbered in the thousands. This store has since closed. *(Chapter 3)*

I shot this photo of my fellow Boy Scouts during a snowshoeing excursion from Crane Lake to Namakin. I almost always took the photographs; that's why I'm not in many of them. *(Chapter 3)*

We spent a week on the Crane Lake to Namakin trip and also used dog sleds. *(Chapter 3)*

In the school band I played percussion. I'm holding a street drum in this photograph, but sometimes I had to carry a marimba home. *(Chapter 4)*

I graduated in May 1944, waiting for my call to join the Army Air Corps. *(Chapter 4)*

Here I am, captain of the school patrol. *(Chapter 4)*

My brother, Bob, our dog, Butch, and I stand in front of my father's 1941 Chevrolet. *(Chapter 4)*

One of my friends is gripping a rope while being pulled down an ice-covered road. *(Chapter 4)*

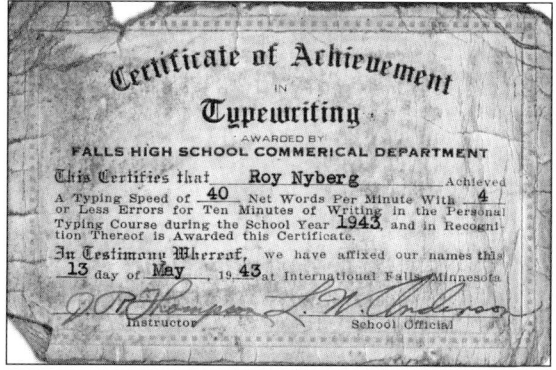

I was honored for typing 40 words per minute with four errors or less in the 11th grade when I began taking commercial or business classes. Remember, this was on an old-fashioned manual typewriter. *(Chapter 4)*

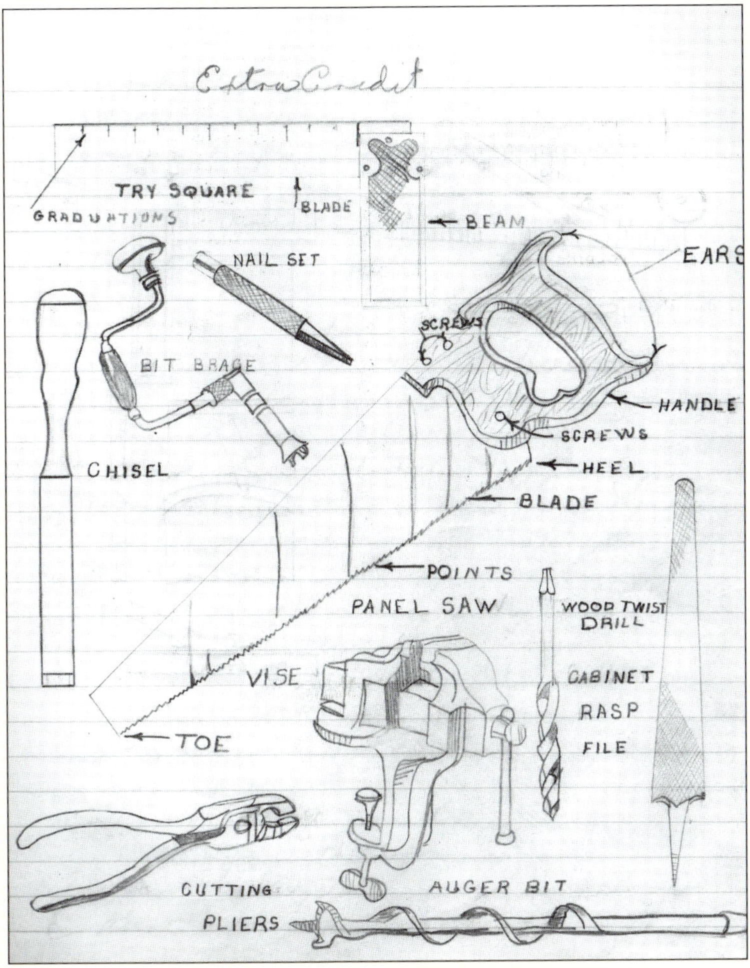

My interest in architecture is evident in these precise drawings for a drafting class.
(Chapter 4)

My family had our photo taken the day I received my uniform. I was 18. I carried a smaller photo with me during my years in the service.
(Chapter 6)

Here I am on my first day in uniform, standing in my Aunt Esther's backyard in St. Paul, Minnesota. *(Chapter 6)*

I'm writing a letter home in front of my tent. I didn't have to use toilet paper this time! *(Chapter 7)*

I'm wearing my work fatigues while aboard the *USS New York University,* sailing in the Mediterranean Sea. *(Chapter 7)*

A guide, a buddy and I (left) stand on the edge of the Mount Vesuvius crater, looking down. A year after it had erupted, it was still so hot that the guide could put paper in a crevice, and it would ignite. *(Chapter 7)*

I am standing on a metal grating. Planes would taxi on that grating at the Naples Air Field. Every morning we would look out at Mount Vesuvius. *(Chapter 7)*

This is me standing in front of the famous Leaning Tower of Pisa. *(Chapter 7)*

I am cleaning the antenna of a C47, using steel wool to remove the debris. I was part of the Mediterranean Air Transport Command. *(Chapter 7)*

I flew over the Leaning Tower of Pisa during a circuit that took us to Naples and Rome. We earned flight pay on those trips. *(Chapter 7)*

I'll never forget kayaking around the Isle of Capri with a buddy. The kayaks' owner wasn't happy with us. *(Chapter 7)*

A bicycle was the means of transportation during a trip to Davos Platz in Switzerland during R&R (rest and recreation). *(Chapter 7)*

This is the flight deck of the aircraft carrier the *USS Franklin D. Roosevelt*. Its first deployment to the Mediterranean was in 1946. *(Chapter 7)*

I'm on the left in this picture taken at Capodichino. Yes, we're drinking beer. *(Chapter 7)*

The USS Missouri is where the treaty was signed with the Japanese, ending World War II. *(Chapter 7)*

While riding on a train in Switzerland, I leaned out the window to take this picture. *(Chapter 7)*

Here I'm rowing in the waters outside the Blue Grotto on the Isle of Capri. *(Chapter 7)*

This is a sacrificial altar in Pompei. I tried to experience as much as I could overseas. *(Chapter 7)*

I am standing by the control panel of a PT boat. *(Chapter 7)*

The best times of my boyhood were spent here at my family's summer home on Rainy Lake. This is the image I kept in my head the whole time I was in the service, and I couldn't wait to return. *(Chapter 8)*

I took this photograph of the Ace Hardware in Hibbing years after I worked there. It was Store No. 74. It has since closed. *(Chapter 9)*

Victor Hultstrand, a St. Louis County commissioner, presents me with the governor's firearms safety award. *(Chapter 10)*

A certificate was presented to me in 1957 for guiding Minnesota's most outstanding firearms safety program. *(Chapter 10)*

Here I am in front of my first store at 2111 S. Minnesota Avenue. I was already making plans to expand. It is Ace Store No. 151. *(Chapter 12)*

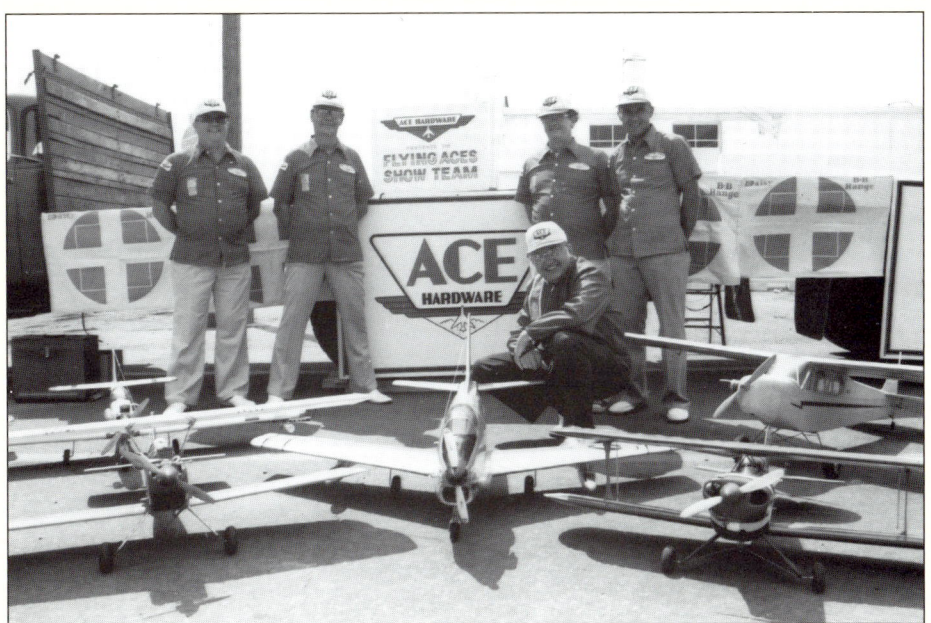

I'm kneeling in front of the Flying Aces and some of their radio-controlled airplanes. We sponsored an air show as a way to promote the store. *(Chapter 13)*

This is the sign that hung in my office for many years, sharing with others the principles that I cherish: exposure, environment and involvement. *(Chapter 14)*

At the annual conventions of the National Retail Hardware Associations, representatives from the different states would be introduced at a grand march. *(Chapter 15)*

Your Business

A VOICE FOR THE LITTLE GUY

When Roy Nyberg speaks, thousands of hardware retailers around the country take notice

By Stephen Asunto

January and February are traditionally the slowest months for the hardware retailer. And if he is nearing retirement, you might expect to find him in his office counting the days as he leans back in a favorite chair.

Such is definitely not the case with Roy Nyberg, president of the National Retail Hardware Association. It was only after several tries that *Hardware Merchandiser* was able to finally coordinate a meeting with the busy hardware spokesperson/businessman in February at his home base in Sioux Falls, S.D.

There, before going off to yet another speaking engagement and tackling a huge backlog of paperwork, Nyberg found a few moments to talk about his life as a retailer, share some thoughts about the hardware industry and discuss his plans for his store and himself when he retires this year.

Roy Nyberg began in the hardware business in 1942 as a high school student working part-time at an Ace Hardware store in International Falls, Minn. There, at the age of 17, he looked ahead to a vocation in hardware. "I made that dream. [I'm] not saying I was setting a goal at that time. But, when I was 17 years of age, I remember very vividly saying that I'm going to have my own hardware store someday."

After serving in the war, Roy came back to Minnesota, took some business courses and began to acquire trade knowledge from his employers and traveling salesmen. Recalls Nyberg, "Where I learned probably more about the hardware business and how not to make mistakes or how to correct mistakes would be from traveling salesmen. We used to have people who'd come in from the store up in Hibbing, [Minn.] and we'd come back after hours and have little store meetings of sorts. Nowadays you call them seminars. That's where we learned [the hardware business]."

In 1958 Nyberg was ready to take advantage of an opportunity to realize his dream and opened his own 4,000 sq. ft. hardware store in Sioux Falls.

As the store grew, Nyberg again sought out experts to help him plan for a new site for his expanding business. He commissioned a survey that suggested locating in a sparse, gravel area on the south side of the city. Several people thought he was crazy to move there. The intersection of 41st and Minnesota is now "the hottest corner in the state of South Dakota," according to Nyberg, who adds, "I had the foresight only because I went to professionals to give me that foresight. You just aren't that knowledgeable in everything that you shouldn't rely on professionals. They can teach you a lot."

With the help of others, and some luck, foresight and planning, Nyberg's Ace Hardware has now expanded to about 30,000 sq. ft. "Never in my fondest imagination did I ever believe that I would have a store of the size that I have now," he exclaims.

Indeed, the present store has departments nearly as large as the first store, which was basically a hardware store with paint, tools, hardware, plumbing and electrical taking up 80% of floor space. Housewares occupied only one wall and sporting goods had all of 12 running feet of wall with some small gondolas on it. In the present store, giftware takes up 2,500 sq. ft., housewares 5,000 sq. ft. and sporting goods 4,000 sq. ft.

When Nyberg compares his old and new stores, three merchandise differences come to mind. "One, you didn't have to worry about colors [or] fashion. You had one Sunbeam mixer— white. You stop to think about just the housewares appliances today [and] not only do you have colors but you've got them doing various things. Back in those days, Toastmaster had the original toaster and was noted probably for the best toaster. Sunbeam had the original mixer and it was the accepted one. And you wouldn't have a wide selection for people, because that's [all] they wanted. Nowadays it seems like when somebody comes out with one product, everybody comes out with their version and take-off on it."

Secondly, Nyberg remarks on the wide variety available today: "There was a day when people would come into a store and ask for something [and the retailer] had enough knowledge about what was available in the whole country from the wholesalers and from the manufacturers that he knew if it was [available or not]."

"Then the third thing would be technology," he continues. "You know, you've got your security alarms, you've got your thermostats. We have become of necessity more technically informed. Nowadays you've got to be an electronic genius."

This magazine article ran in Hardware Merchandiser magazine when I became president of the National Retail Hardware Association. (Chapter 15)

Here are four generations of Nybergs: daughter, Jody; my mother, Helen Wirt Nyberg; me, and my grandmother, Jessie Lee Wirt. My mother was dressed up for her installation as a worthy matron with the Order of Eastern Star. *(Chapter 16)*

The Ace Hardware store in International Falls before it closed. The glass I cut for the store's bins was used for more than 60 years. *(Chapter 3)*

Me in my Boy Scout uniform, showing the badges that I earned. The hat with a brim was one of scouting's first official hats and belonged to an uncle. *(Chapter 3)*

My brother, Bob; his blind date, Marge Murdock; Rodora Dokken, and I stand on Lyndale Avenue in front of an ice cream shop after the Aquatennial Parade. This was my first date with Rodora, and she didn't want to go alone. *(Chapter 8)*

A family photo on our wedding day. From left: Elvin Dokken, Florence Dokken, Rodora, me, Helen Nyberg and Otto Nyberg. *(Chapter 8)*

Rodora and I were married in Gol Lutheran Church just outside Kenyon, Minnesota, on September 16, 1950. *(Chapter 8)*

Rodora and I are preparing to leave for our honeymoon in the Black Hills. *(Chapter 8)*

We honeymooned at the lodge along Sylvan Lake in the Black Hills. *(Chapter 9)*

In this photo from the late 1960s, I'm riding in a wagon during the Crazy Daze parade on Main Avenue, wearing two diapers. I brought the idea of a crazy days sale to Sioux Falls. *(Chapter 12)*

One of my hardware store promotions received national attention: I put a lawnmower atop a huge pile of snow. *(Chapter 12)*

This view of the Southway Shopping Center shows everything from the A&W Root Beer Stand to Sam's Super Valu. *(Chapter 12)*

I decorated the store one Halloween, covering all the windows. The bureaucrats didn't like it – too much advertising! *(Chapter 12)*

My secretary, Donna Souter, had to sit on a step ladder, my office was so small and crammed full of stuff. *(Chapter 12)*

My employees stand by the sign we erected to tell people what was coming to 41st Street and Minnesota Avenue. *(Chapter 13)*

Taking part in the groundbreaking for a new store at 41st Street and Minnesota Avenue are Rodora, Harriet Kaiser, me and Ernie Kaiser. Ernie was my partner for only a short time before he died of leukemia. *(Chapter 13)*

My new 70-foot-tall sign is going up. I made sure you could see it for blocks away – from a competitor's front door, in fact! I called it "The tallest sign in the sky!" *(Chapter 13)*

This photo of Nyberg's Ace Hardware at 41st Street and Minnesota Avenue was taken in the late 1960s. *(Chapter 13)*

As one of our promotions, we would have a flea market in the parking lot. People would come down on Saturday to reserve a place. *(Chapter 13)*

I am waiting on my first walk-in cash customer at the new store, Don Swanson of Hutton-Tufty car dealership. *(Chapter 13)*

Rodora and I are standing with some of the flowers we received for our grand opening. *(Chapter 13)*

"Who's Next Please?" is a book that I was instrumental in getting published. It has helped many retailers plan for their future retirement, and the Nybergs are featured in it. *(Chapter 15)*

I put myself on Mount Rushmore as a promotion the year I became president of the National Retail Hardware Association. My slogan was "Roy's one of the boys!" *(Chapter 15)*

We bought this 15-foot Forester trailer to take us to national conventions from our friend, Louis Peloquin, after we moved to Sioux Falls. Louis is on the right; another friend, Boyd Angen, is on the left. *(Chapter 15)*

This is the year I was president of the National Retail Hardware Association. I'm speaking from the rostrum. Notice the U.S. and Canada flags; we had members in both countries. *(Chapter 15)*

One year the National Retail Hardware Association's convention theme was country-western. Rodora hated it those few times I grew a beard. *(Chapter 15)*

John Meyer, president of the South Dakota Retailers Association, presented Kevin and me with a plaque after Nyberg's Ace Hardware was named state retailer of the year in 2010. *(Chapter 15)*

Here, Rodora and I are at another NRHA convention. The banquets were formal affairs: long dresses for the women and tuxedos for the men. *(Chapter 15)*

Our children and in-laws from Sioux Falls also attended the SDRA event. From left: Bruce and Marin Huber, Rodora, me, Linda and Kevin Nyberg, and Nancy and Rick Swanson. *(Chapter 15)*

Our kids enjoyed going to the Dokken farm to visit Rodora's folks. Rodora's father, Elroy, is driving the tractor. *(Chapter 16)*

My dad hewed the trees to make this path to the Nyberg cabin on Rainy Lake. It was so muddy during this visit that we had to walk, not drive. *(Chapter 16)*

Our grandkids are shown in this 2009 photo. From left: Laura Swanson, Karin Swanson, Jennifer Swanson, Jon-Erik Huber, Erik Nyberg, Camryn Huber, Kelly Nyberg, Karmen Nyberg and Kirsten Nyberg. Allison Huber is between us. *(Chapter 16)*

Lou Knobe (left) and Rick Knobe (right), the former mayor of Sioux Falls, came with me to the Boundary Waters. We're standing on an island occupied by Dorothy Molson, the "root beer lady" of Ely, Minnesota. *(Chapter 17)*

To make sure the bears couldn't get into our supplies in northern Minnesota, we would hang the gear in the trees. I learned this as a Scout and taught it to the others. *(Chapter 17)*

When I took high school kids to northern Minnesota, we would fill the canoes with enough gear to last a week. *(Chapter 17)*

South Dakota allows youngsters to hunt a week ahead of the regular season. We let kids and their dads come to our hunting lodge to take advantage of the plentiful pheasants in that area. *(Chapter 17)*

Shogun: a hunting partnership of five friends for other friends to enjoy. And there are no release birds! *(Chapter 17)*

In 2006, I made one last trip to my beloved Boundary Waters in northern Minnesota. I was 80, and so I carried some gear but not the canoe! *(Chapter 17)*

My granddaughter Kelly Nyberg, then two years old, and I dressed up for Halloween in 1989. But I wore my clown outfit much more often as a member of the El Riad Shrine clowns. *(Chapter 18)*

Here I am on the left with fellow El Riad clown James K. Pentico. My forte was when young girls on the parade route seemed glum, I'd say, "Smile if you're cute," and they would! *(Chapter 18)*

I am now an honorary clown and remain a proud member of the El Riad Shrine. *(Chapter 18)*

After retirement, Rodora and I traveled a lot. During our trip to western China, we met a woman who had had a series of metal rings attached to her neck, stretching it out. Only girls born on Wednesday were "lucky" enough to have this done. *(Chapter 20)*

In 1997 at an outdoor market in western China, we found a dentist with a table and chair – in the open – preparing to work on one of the minority tribe members. *(Chapter 20)*

I photographed this polar bear on a trip to Churchill, Manitoba, Canada, in 1997. Rodora planned this trip, and it still remains her favorite. *(Chapter 20)*

Here we are in Thailand, where an elephant was our transportation across the water and through the forest. *(Chapter 20)*

During a trip to the Marshall Islands, I caught this fish. Actually, the guides snagged it, and I reeled it in. The fish were sold to the restaurants, and I think we had it for supper that night. *(Chapter 20)*

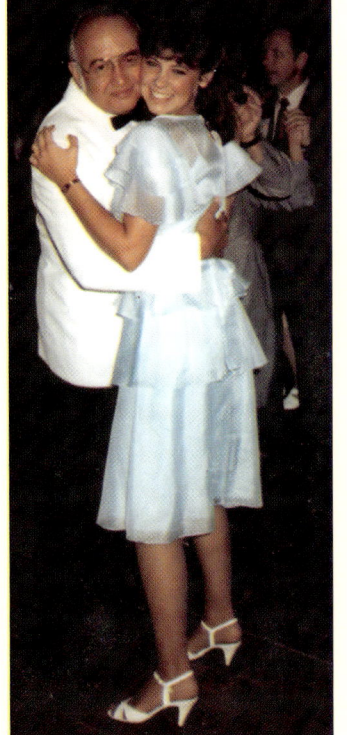

My son, Kevin, paddles a canoe on the Big Sioux River in the early 1960s. *(Chapter 19)*

Marin and I always danced to the same tune at the annual conventions: "In the Mood." It was our song! *(Chapter 21)*

All of us attended the grand opening of the Ace Hardware Store at 41st Street and Sertoma Avenue. From left: Marin, Kevin, Nancy, Jody, Rodora and me. *(Chapter 21)*

Rodora and I have chosen the marker for our burial plot in Woodlawn Cemetery – so I, a good Swede, will be buried under a Norwegian pearl granite stone!